Audio-Visual Techniques
In Teaching Foreign Languages

Revised Edition

Audio-Visual Techniques

In Teaching

Foreign Languages

A PRACTICAL HANDBOOK BY

THEODORE HUEBENER

Professor of Languages,
Fairleigh Dickinson University
Formerly Director of Foreign Languages
in the Schools of the City of New York

REVISED EDITION

New York · NEW YORK UNIVERSITY PRESS
London · UNIVERSITY OF LONDON PRESS LIMITED
1967

Preface
to the First Edition

udio-visual devices of the simpler kind have been available for a long time, yet strange to say, foreign language teachers have made comparatively little use of them. This is all the more deplorable in view of the fact that they lend themselves so well to that area and can strengthen the linguistic phase as well as enrich the cultural phase of language teaching. In this connection teachers have invariably thought of the latter first. A phonograph record was to be used for giving a sample of the music of the foreign people; the film was always shown to depict life in the foreign country.

Within recent years, however, the importance of audio-visual devices in teaching the language has come to the fore. In fact, the very latest materials are primarily concerned with speech. This development is a direct outgrowth of the urgency of a thorough knowledge of foreign languages on the part of our technicians and representatives abroad due to the assumption of cultural, as well as political and military, leadership in the Western world by the United States.

The most realistic evidence of this importance of a knowledge of foreign languages is the National Educational Defense Act which has provided millions of dollars for the improvement of instruction in science, mathematics, and foreign languages. On the secondary level the Act specifically recommends that the moneys be expended for the purchase of orthophonic equipment suitable for language instruction.

Another striking fact is the recent rapid development of

mechanical devices, both visual and audial, for the learning of languages. The market is full of a vast array of phonograph records, playback machines, projectors, filmstrips, tape recorders, microphones, repeating machines, motion pictures, and laboratory equipment. The teacher is faced with a veritable *embarras de richesses*. How is he to use it effectively?

To provide the answer to this question is the primary aim of the present volume. It is designed as a practical handbook for the teacher of foreign languages in the use of audio-visual devices.

After a brief description of each type of equipment, a detailed discussion of various procedures and techniques is presented. An attempt is made to cover the entire area of foreign language instruction, from the lowest grades to college.

Not only the latest and more elaborate machines are described, but also the very simplest devices, since these are generally the more readily available and the more useful to the teacher in the elementary grades. In fact, many of these are so simple and so obvious that they have not been fully exploited. The many suggestions given should lead the resourceful teacher to develop further devices and techniques appropriate for a given learning situation.

In order to be really helpful, procedures are not only described in general terms but detailed outlines of specific lessons are given for each device. In fact, illustrative lessons are provided in French, German, Italian, Latin, and Spanish.

The appendix contains an up-to-date bibliography. Since the field is so new, there is very little on foreign languages. Most of the books on audio-visual instruction barely mention that field. The best material is still to be found in folders, reports, and magazine articles. There is also a rather comprehensive list of sources of the various types of materials.

The author wishes to express his thanks to several people who generously gave their permission to include certain materials in this book. Among these are Dr. William H. Bristow, Director of Curriculum Research, and Dr. Edward Bernard, Director of Audio-Visual Instruction. The description of tape recording and of the use of the tape recorder is based on a report issued by Dr. Bristow. It was prepared by Sarah Lorge of the Audio-Visual Bureau and Co-ordinator of the Language Laboratory Project—a research study co-ordinated by Dr. Bernard. The list of approved phonograph records is based on a compilation prepared by Helen Klug, Foreign

Language Supervisor of the Bureau of Audio-Visual Instruction. The television programs cited as illustrations are under the direction of James Macandrew, Director of the Regents Educational Television Project.

We hope that this book will prove practical and inspirational to the teacher of foreign languages, especially with reference to the use of audio-visual techniques.

T.H.
1960

Preface
to the Second Edition

Since the publication of the first edition of this book a number of remarkable improvements have been made in several technical devices used in teaching. Tape recording has been made easier and cheaper. Practically all the newer basic textbooks in foreign languages are provided with tapes, and publishers are inclined to permit teachers to reproduce them for classroom use. The quality of the tapes has been improved.

The language laboratory, which has undergone several physical changes, is being more widely used, although the tendency is to make use of simpler equipment. This involves the mobile lab which is far more economical and practical, since it can be introduced at any time into any classroom.

The effectiveness of the laboratory, especially for the teaching of auditory comprehension has received a great impetus through the greatly increased production of usable selections, drill exercises and tests. These are discussed in the completely revised chapter on the laboratory.

Television, especially the closed circuit, is being used more and more for educational purposes. Even more revolutionary are the introduction of programmed instruction and the teaching machine into the classroom. Thus far little has been done with these devices with respect to foreign language teaching. The use of the machine will be extremely limited because of its prohibitive cost. And a good course in programmed instruction in foreign languages has yet to be constructed.

Not to be overlooked are the extensive modifications which have been made in the theory and practice of the audio-lingual approach. One that is particularly significant in connection with the use of technical devices is the realization that the stress on the audial must not exclude the visual. The film and the motion picture have as useful a function to perform as the tape-recorder and the earphone.

One the whole, the average foreign language teacher will—for some time to come—still have to rely on the simpler and less expensive audio-visual devices and materials. How to use these more effectively is the subject of this book.

T.H.

1966

Contents

APPENDIX

Audio-Visual Techniques
In Teaching Foreign Languages
Revised Edition

[I]

Introduction

HISTORICAL BACKGROUND

THE FIRST IMPORTANT EDUCATOR to appreciate the value of visual aids in teaching was Comenius, the seventeenth-century exponent of sense realism. With his unusually keen mind he anticipated many of the basic principles and practices in common use today. For example, in his *Great Didactic,* published in 1632, in which he developed his educational theories, he recommends among other things attractive classrooms, maximum sense appeal, and good textbooks. The last two led directly to the illustrated textbook, which is another of the significant contributions of Comenius.

In his *Orbis Pictus,* which was used up to modern times, he incorporated ideas which are still effective in the construction of schoolbooks and the teaching of foreign languages. Latin, which was the all-important language of the times, was to be learned through the vernacular; hence sentences were arranged in parallel columns. Numbers placed beside given words and expressions referred to objects, persons, and actions with the corresponding numbers in a woodcut at the top of the page. The *Orbis Pictus* was the

1

first illustrated book, and a good job it was. Every picture was interesting but it also served directly a serious pedagogic purpose. Comenius employed three other important principles of effective language learning: (a) the foreign language, in this case Latin, was to be taught as a living tongue, (b) the vocabulary was to consist of everyday words and expressions to make the child acquainted with natural phenomena, daily life and occupations, and (c) the text in the foreign language and the vernacular translation were placed side by side. This latter method has only recently come into vogue again.

In his *Janua Linguarum Reserata,* or "Gate of Language Unlocked," Comenius outlined the ideas and theories which were put into practice in the *Orbis Pictus.* The important basic principle underlying his books and procedures is that of environmental vocabulary, that is, the learner's seeing of objects, persons, and activities immediately around him. The stress here was, of course, on the visual; the teacher was really the only auditory medium available.

Comenius has deservedly been called "the prince of schoolmasters" and his *Great Didactic* one of the outstanding educational works of all time. Strange to say, however, his theoretical writings remained unknown and had no immediate influence either on elementary education or on the teaching of languages. Not until the protagonists of the direct method appeared over two hundred years later were his theories acclaimed and put into practice.

Some of these that apply to audio-visual methods are the following:

1. Education should be adapted to the age and capacity of the child.
2. A graduated series of textbooks and illustrative material are absolute essentials for effective teaching.
3. Fatigue should be avoided.
4. Class instruction is preferable to individual teaching.
5. Printed books should be used instead of copied materials.
6. All subjects should be illustrated pictorially, if possible.
7. Actual objects and things should be studied first.
8. Examples should come before rules.
9. The minds of pupils should be prepared for new subject matter.
10. A pleasant atmosphere should prevail in the classroom.

AUDIO-VISUAL AIDS AND LEARNING

THE USE OF AUDIO-VISUAL MATERIALS and methods increases the effectiveness of learning by helping the pupil to assimilate ideas in a more meaningful and interesting manner. Through the appeal to eye and ear they provide for a systematic improvement of knowledge and skills, as well as a favorable influence on attitudes and appreciations. These objectives, of course, are attained only if the most suitable materials for a given learning situation are selected and if the pupils are prepared in advance.

Each type of audio-visual aid has its place and each has its limitations. It is best to learn by actual experience, but since the possibilities in the classroom are limited, resort must be had to carefully planned vicarious experience. This is provided by audio-visual aids.

What Audio-Visual Aids Can Do. Any audio-visual aid, then, is a substitute for actual experience. However, since it is planned, concentrated, and enlivened by means of the latest technical devices, it can accomplish effectively most of the objectives of education.

The proper use of audio-visual aids should

1. Reduce the danger of verbalism.
2. Increase better understanding.
3. Arouse interest in research.
4. Develop power of oral and written communication.
5. Encourage pupil participation.
6. Build up clearer and richer concepts.
7. Provide for group thinking and planning.
8. Train in efficient work and study habits.
9. Instill favorable attitudes.
10. Foster the appreciation of beauty.

AVAILABLE AUDIO-VISUAL MATERIALS

WITH THE RAPID ADVANCES that have been made in the development of orthophonic equipment, there is now a wide variety of audio-visual aids available for use in the school or college. In fact, the extent of commercial materials and machines is now so extensive that the teacher is faced with an *embarras de richesse*. It is no longer a question of looking for devices but rather of being guided in making a wise selection.

The audio-visual aids available for the foreign language teacher may be grouped as follows:

A. VISUAL

1. Flat materials: pictures, flash cards, maps, charts, cardboard figures.
2. Three-dimensional: puppets, dolls, models, dioramas.
3. Projected materials: films, filmstrips, motion pictures, television.

B. AUDITORY

1. Phonograph discs.
2. Tape recorder and tapes.
3. Radio.
4. Motion picture with sound.
5. Television.

The apogee in orthophonic devices and materials is attained in the language laboratory which attempts to make use of all possible mechanical aids in developing facility in comprehension and in speech.

A New Emphasis in Language Learning. The marked stress on learning to speak a foreign language has led to the wide use of mechanical devices for recording and reproducing sound. But, strangely enough, the use of such aids has affected not only the methodology involved but the very thinking on the nature of language. The following assumptions underlie the new techniques:

1. Language is essentially speech, and speech is basically communication by sounds.

2. Sounds made by the voice are far more complex and go far beyond the symbols of the international phonetic alphabet. There are many delicate nuances and inflections, grunts and puffs, which occur in daily speech but are not represented by any graphic symbol.

3. The graphic symbol, therefore, is inadequate to record the complete and rich pattern of human speech. Letters cannot represent the various shadings of sounds. These must be learned by imitation.

4

4. The best model to imitate is the native speaker or someone with a near-native accent.

5. Speaking a language is a skill. A skill is acquired by much repetition. It is primarily a neuromuscular and not an intellectual process.

6. The opportunity offered by the traditional classroom for practice of a foreign language is very inadequate.

7. Orthophonic devices and, particularly, the language laboratory provide adequate facilities for practice.

[II]

Visual Materials
& Techniques

THE USE OF VISUAL AIDS

As has been pointed out, the use of visual aids in the classroom is nothing essentially new, for these include everything in the way of illustrative materials except the textbook. They are employed to take the place of the actual experience that cannot be had in the classroom. Audio-visual aids provide a contrived experience.

Since an attempt is made to encompass almost the entire range of illustrative materials—visual aids, auditory aids, and combinations of the two—a more expressive term would be "scientific aids to learning." Of course, in every instance there is the material or the machine and the method of using it.

VISUAL VERSUS AUDIAL. Still pictures are simpler than auditory materials since the more elementary ones do not depend upon any me-

6

chanical device. Pictures, drawings, charts, models, dioramas, etc. are simply displayed. The impression is probably more lasting, too, because attention can be centered for any desired length of time on a still object.

The impression is undoubtedly deeper, for most people seem to be visual-minded. Formerly it was thought that over 80 per cent of what we learned came through the eye. Experimentation, however, has led to the belief that all senses are more or less involved in learning. In fact, they are so interlinked that it is difficult to separate one from the other. The multiple-sense appeal theory rests on a sound base. In this connection foreign language teachers may accept one of the older ways of teaching spelling in the vernacular. The pupil heard the word, wrote it on paper, pronounced it as he was writing it, and then wrote it in the air. The only sense not involved was that of smell.

The eye, however, may still be considered of primary importance. It is undoubtedly the most impressionable of all the senses.

Originally, man relied solely on pictorial representation for keeping records. Before the alphabet came the pictogram and the hieroglyph. Gradually writing became more and more stylized; the picture turned into a symbol. Language became more abstract. Therefore, in order to enrich and vivify concepts it is important to include a maximum number of things or representations of things.

The importance of vision in forming lasting impression cannot be overemphasized. Experimental evidence clearly demonstrates the great importance of visual aids in teaching.

The Foreign Language Room

ATMOSPHERE. Learning is increased by favorable conditions. The learning of a foreign language is promoted by an attractive foreign atmosphere. This can be created by the careful planning of suitable room decorations.

DECORATIONS. With reference to classroom displays the average foreign language teacher undoubtedly thinks first of the aesthetic side. He puts up such materials as will produce a pleasing effect on the eye. That is perfectly justified: the classroom should not be somber and forbidding, but cheerful, attractive, and beautiful.

The decorations, however, should serve another purpose. They should be of such a nature that they can be used in the teaching of the language. In other words, the materials on display should be not only aesthetic but also pedagogic.

STANDARDS. Just filling up a room with a lot of pictures, charts, and models, even if colorful, will not achieve any educational purpose. In fact, a plethora of unrelated materials may prove to be a distraction. Thought should be given to the suitability of what is put up. The following criteria for judging the material will be useful; the teacher should ask himself:

1. *Is it aesthetic?* That is, is it pleasing, beautiful? This is particularly important in the case of posters and framed pictures which are likely to remain on the wall. These should be significant, of lasting value and interest. The colorful poster will catch the eye of other teachers and pupils using the foreign language room. Unconsciously their interest will be aroused. Here is a chance to publicize the foreign language.

2. *Is it in good taste?* The poster may be colorful, technically perfect, and quite attractive but not suitable for the classroom. This applies, for example, to liquor and cigarette advertisements. It would rule out travel publicity stressing the night life of the foreign country. It is also desirable not to overemphasize through displays certain aspects of the foreign civilization which are cruel or bloody, according to American standards. There is, for example, the bullfight, which is the subject of many attractive posters but is, after all, a gory spectacle. Many Spanish teachers who feature it in their room decorations seem to be unaware of the fact that in the majority of Latin-American countries the *corrida de toros* is forbidden.

In the French classroom one often sees little models, carefully prepared by students, depicting an execution by guillotine, with a generous amount of red ink to represent pools of blood. This is not a desirable display.

3. *Is it timely?* The displays should be changed occasionally to conform with the march of time and the seasons. A pupil does not get a correct impression of Paris by looking daily at a picture representing the Opéra in 1898 with horse-drawn carriages standing in front of it. Also, it is entirely out of place to have pictures of Christmas on the walls in June. The bulletin board should be a special concern in this regard.

4. *Is it pedagogically useful?* A classroom may be attractively decorated and still the materials may be of such a nature that they are

8

never referred to by the teacher. Some things, of course, are pedagogic rather than decorative, as, for example, the clock dial, the map, and the pronunciation charts.

TYPES OF MATERIALS

THE KINDS OF MATERIALS that may be put on display in a classroom fall into various categories. There are large and small items; more or less permanent and temporary; pictorial and lettered material; purchased, and that prepared by pupils; flat and projected.

1. LARGER, MORE PERMANENT DISPLAYS. Posters and pictures, especially those that are framed, are in this category. Posters, which almost without exception are in color, may be obtained from travel and government tourist agencies. Some of the posters are veritable works of art. In most cases they may be had free; in others there is a charge of from 50 cents to $1.

For the posters it is best to select those that show characteristic scenes and typical buildings in the foreign country. For example:

France. Scenes in Normandy, Brittany, Alsace, Southern France; buildings and monuments in Paris, Rouen, Lyons, Marseilles, Nice; important cathedrals; châteaux along the Loire.

Germany. Scenes along the Rhine, in North Germany, the Black Forest, in Bavaria; buildings and monuments in Berlin, Hamburg, Frankfurt, Munich; important cathedrals and castles.

Italy. Scenes in North Italy, the mountains, along the sea, in Sicily; buildings and monuments in Rome, Florence, Venice, Genoa, Naples; important cathedrals.

Spain. Scenes in northern, middle, and southern Spain; buildings and monuments in Madrid, Burgos, Barcelona, Seville; important cathedrals; the Alhambra.

Latin America. Scenes in Caracas, Bogotá, Lima, Santiago, Buenos Aires; the Indians; cathedrals; the Andes.

All of the above are attractive and also lend themselves as illustrative material for given lessons.

The framed pictures—there will probably be room for only a limited number—may continue the themes of the posters or, better, present reproductions of famous paintings by foreign artists.

An excellent idea is to group such pictures by painters. They may be displayed successively, say for a month or two each.

Another scheme that may be followed is to use the pictures or the portraits of eminent men and women of the foreign country. To make these all the more useful, it would be well to label them in fairly large letters. The dates of birth and death may be added.

2. ARTIFACTS. Teachers who have traveled and brought back interesting artifacts often put these on display in the classroom. There are the sombrero and the serape from Mexico; the fans and mantillas from Spain; the Hummel figures from Germany; the costume dolls from France. Such items may be attached to boards or heavy cardboard and then hung up, or put into glass wall display cases if these are available in the school. Such material, too, should be labeled. In the more affluent neighborhoods, students may be asked to contribute if they or their parents have traveled.

3. FLAGS. A flag of the foreign country is a suitable decoration. In the case of the Spanish room there is, of course, the possibility of displaying not only the flag of Spain but those of all the Latin-American countries.

4. PROVERBS. Another item that should be included in every foreign language classroom is a collection of neatly lettered proverbs. The lettering should be fairly large, stylistically correct, and uniform. Proverbs—or any other inscription, for that matter—in script are not to be recommended.

5. CHARTS AND INSTRUCTIONAL MATERIAL. The pronunciation chart plays an important role in the French classroom, less so in the case of the other languages. The charts can be homemade or bought.

Every language room should have a clock dial available for the lesson on time.

A daily calendar with an inset for the date of the day is a useful device. A monitor can take care of the change of date.

6. MAPS. A good map of the foreign country is essential. If a large roller map is not obtainable, the teacher can secure a smaller one and mount it. Maps drawn by pupils should be accurate. Maps, as well as illustrations, can be enlarged by pupils by using proportional squares. These may be superimposed with tracing paper or drawn directly on the original. Another good method is the use of the pantograph. In any case, irregular, incorrect, and distorted maps done by pupils should not be put on display.

7. PUPIL'S WORK. In addition to maps, many teachers like to display the work of pupils in labeled illustrations, scrapbooks, copies of pictures, models, etc. Only the best of such material should be shown.

Entailing more work and research are models and dioramas representing scenes in the foreign country or historic events. A favorite in the French class is the Eiffel Tower. Such an activity can be arranged as a term project and the best work may be displayed in a glass case in the hall or in the school library.

Labeling. A special feature of the foreign language room is the labeling of objects. This has great pedagogic value, for by looking at the foreign name of the object, day after day, it is indelibly impressed on the student's mind.

The objects that may be labeled are the wall, the window, the door, the closet, the bookshelf, the teacher's deck, the map, etc. Portraits of eminent men and women should bear their names; reproductions of famous paintings should bear captions. All of these, of course, should be neat, fairly large, clear, and uniform in style.

In elementary and beginning classes the labels prepare for the prereading stage. When the pupils begin to write they can be asked to label pictures in scrap- and workbooks, on mimeographed sheets; they can also label simple drawings on the board. This will be the first step toward more extensive writing.

The Bulletin Board. Every foreign language room should have a bulletin board. If carefully planned and skillfully managed, it becomes a wonderful device for motivation, for teaching, and for maintaining interest. It should not consist of a disconnected jumble of pictures, clippings, and news items, but should be related to the classwork.

Primarily, of course, many of the items will be in the foreign language. However, news items in English treating important current events also will be included. The endeavor should be to present what is significant, timely, and interesting. A comic strip in the foreign language may be posted, now and then, to hold the interest of the less academic, but in general the tone of the bulletin board should be dignified. The news items will be about important political and economic events; happenings in the world of art and music; comments on writers and poets; possibly the description of

Visual Materials and Techniques / 11

a disaster, if one has occurred. Interesting items about school, youth, sport, festivities, etc. are suitable.

The clippings may be contributed by various members of the class. If the teacher or the class has a subscription to a foreign newspaper or magazine, this should furnish a good source of clippings. Students may alternate in taking care of the bulletin board or a committee may be assigned for the entire term.

The teacher will draw attention to particularly interesting items and will use them for oral and written reports.

The physical arrangements are, of course, important. Pictures and clippings should be placed neatly. Spacing should be watched. If one theme is being treated—"Christmas in France," "Holy Week in Spain," or "The October Festival in Munich"—a neatly lettered caption should be placed at the top. For special events and anniversaries of great men the idea of a single theme is especially desirable.

The bulletin board can be used for the display of items of almost any type, as for example:

Announcements	Drawings
Booklets, travel brochures	Graphs
Bulletins	Notices
Charts	Pictures
Diagrams	Pamphlets
Maps	Photographs
News clippings	Postcards

Considerable thought should be given to the planning of a bulletin board. Various factors involved are:

1. The collection of material. As it will consist largely of newspaper and magazine clippings, it will be taken from a number of given publications. These will include Sunday magazine sections, *Life, Time, Look,* and similar weeklies and monthlies in the foreign language.

2. Each item should be neatly trimmed. If it is a picture, it may be mounted.

3. If a general theme is developed for a longer display, there ought to be a neatly lettered title.

4. Where captions are missing, they should be supplied.

5. To make the bulletin board attractive, color should be used.

6. All the material should be arranged in a neat, orderly, and attractive manner.

7. Students should be encouraged to look at the bulletin board.

8. The teacher may refer to the bulletin board in the course of the lesson.

9. Displays should be changed at regular intervals.

Maps. Another form of chart that should be available in the foreign language classroom is a good map of the foreign country.

It should be used (a) to point out the location of places mentioned in reading passages or occurring in the lesson, and (b) to present a sequential treatment of the geography and culture of the foreign country.

The first is simple enough. Avignon occurs in the reading passage and in the song.

"Où est Avignon? Monsieur Jones, montrez-nous Avignon sur la carte."

Jones goes to the map, points to the place name, and says, "Voilà Avignon."

This may be elaborated to "Avignon est situé sur le Rhône" or "À Avignon il y a un pont dont nous chantons une chanson."

More formal map study will confine itself to one section or region, for example, Brittany. The teacher asks questions about the boundaries, the coast line, the topography, the names of important cities, etc.

All place names are located on the map. But the concepts should be enriched. In order that they may become more than mere names, the teacher should show the pupils pictures of the places mentioned. In that way they will get some idea as to what Quimper, Vannes, Rennes, and St.-Malo look like. Perhaps there is a poster of Mont-St.-Michel on the wall to which the teacher can refer, even though the island does not technically belong to Brittany.

In addition to the showing of pictures, costume dolls may be shown. If a model of a Breton home is available, that would be good too. In any event some interesting fact should be learned in connection with each town, village, or region.

Brittany—Britain, Britons; the Celts; their language; their religion (ardently Catholic); character of the people.

Rennes—where Dreyfus trial took place in Palace of Justice.

Vannes—famous naval battle mentioned by Caesar. Benjamin Franklin landed here on his first visit to France; it took him thirteen days to get to Paris.

Visual Materials and Techniques / 1 3

Quimper—famous for pottery. This type of ceramic sold in New England, where it is called "Guimper."

St.-Malo—haven of pirates in the past.

Brest—American troops landed here in World War I.

Pupils are frequently encouraged to draw maps, with very indifferent results. Outlines are distorted, lettering is poor, place names are misspelled. Such maps should not be put on display. A map is a matter not of freehand drawing and of self-expression but of accurate draftsmanship and careful lettering.

Accuracy can be attained in any desirable size by using the proportional square method.

THE PROPORTIONAL SQUARE METHOD. Frequently an outline drawing or map is a useful visual device. In many cases the illustration is too small to be seen by the entire class. But there is an easy way of enlarging it to any desired size. That is done by using the proportional square method.

Horizontal and vertical lines, a half inch or an inch apart, are drawn on the picture. Or, if the photograph or picture is not to be disfigured, the lines can be superimposed on tissue or tracing paper. An equal number of squares are then laid out on the blackboard or

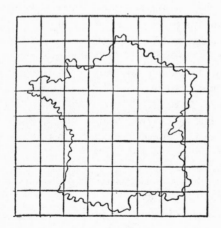

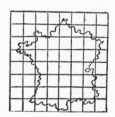

THE PROPORTIONAL SQUARE

on a larger sheet of paper. They can be doubled or tripled or increased to any desirable size. The contour of the map or picture to be copied is then drawn in proportion in each square. Even the person with little skill in drawing will be able to produce something acceptable.

This method is highly recommended for the drawing of maps, where accuracy is of prime importance.

STANDARDS. For optimum effectiveness, a map should meet certain standards. These are:

1. Simplicity and clarity. If a map is cluttered up with place names and detail, it will be hard to read, especially at a distance.
2. Accuracy. The map should be accurate. This, however, does not mean that every last hamlet and every brook has to be shown. For ordinary purposes, the names of the chief cities, rivers, and mountains will do. The scale, of course, should be correct.
3. Adequate size. The map should be large enough to be visible from the back of the room.
4. Good color. The colors should be pleasing.
5. Proper physical make-up. The map should be well mounted and housed in a dustproof case with a spring roller.

The Pronunciation Chart. The pronunciation chart, unfortunately, is not used very much nowadays. Like the teaching of phonetics, it seems to have lapsed into desuetude. It is, however, of considerable value for corrective exercises in pronunciation, especially in French. During the first year the teacher must be constantly on the alert to correct mispronunciation of vowels and diphthongs.

If a set of pronunciation charts is on display in the room, they can be referred to at any moment. In fact, having them in view every day is psychologically good, for the impression is heightened by constant repetition.

There is no need to letter such charts. A set of fourteen or fifteen, neatly printed, can be purchased at a nominal price.

The Clock Dial. For the teaching of time, a clock dial is indispensable. This useful device can be purchased or can easily be made of cardboard.

Like the flash card it can be manipulated by the teacher or by a pupil. The standard question, of course, is, "What time is it?" "Quelle heure est-il?" "Wieviel Uhr ist es?" "Che ora è?" "¿Qué hora es?"

The steps in teaching time are almost obvious. The procedure is from the simple to the complex.

ILLUSTRATIVE LESSON

Telling Time

(Spanish)

LA HORA

1. The numbers 1–12 are rapidly reviewed orally. They are applied by having the pupils give the even hours.

> ¿Qué hora es?
> Son las tres. Son las seis. Son las dos.

2. The numbers 1–60, by fives, are reviewed. The teacher shows how minutes are added after the hour.

> Son las dos y veinte.
> Son las dos y veinte y cinco.

3. All the numbers from 1 to 60 are reviewed. Uneven combinations are now used.

> Son las cuatro y veinte y ocho.

4. The principle of adding and deducting minutes is taught. *Cuarto* and *media* are taught.

> Son las ocho menos cinco.

5. Finally, expressions like *en punto, mediodía, medianoche, de la mañana, de la tarde,* and *de la noche* are taught.

The question ¿Qué hora es? can be replaced by reference to the day's activities.

> ¿A qué hora
> > se levanta Vd.?
> > se desayuna Vd.?
> > va Vd. a la escuela?
> > tiene Vd. su lección de español?
> > almuerza Vd.?
> > vuelve Vd. a casa? etc.

THE BLACKBOARD

THE SIMPLEST and most immediate visual aid is the blackboard. It is so common and so universally used that it is taken for granted. In fact, it is even overlooked as a visual aid of prime importance.

Strangely enough, it did not come into general use until the nineteenth century. There is a picture of a blackboard in the *Orbis Pictus* published in 1658, which shows that Comenius—that educator-genius who anticipated a number of important teaching devices and principles two centuries ago—realized its value. Like most of his valuable contributions to language teaching, it does not seem to have become popular until much later. The blackboard is not mentioned in American educational literature before 1820. It was Horace Mann who observed its use in European schools and was so impressed with its effectiveness that he recommended it with enthusiasm as an instrument of instruction. It became a favorite first in mathematics classes and was then used in other subjects. Today a classroom without a blackboard is unthinkable.

Types of Blackboards. Various materials have been used in the construction of the blackboard. Generally it has consisted of a wooden surface painted or stained black—hence the name "blackboard." Since other materials and colors are now used, many educational writers are using the term "chalkboard." This has not, however, become popular as yet; the average teacher still calls it the blackboard.

In Europe the board painted black and the wet rag for erasures has prevailed, since it is cheapest. In the United States the more expensive medium of slate has been in general use. It has proved to be an excellent graphic medium. More recently etched plate glass stained with black pigment has been introduced.

The color of the blackboard is usually black or gray, and the chalk used is usually white. The colors, however, have been reversed: there is the white board on which black crayon is used. Through experimentation it has been found that blue chalk on a yellow board lessens eyestrain. Also, the difference in color adds a note of cheerfulness to the classroom. This fact, together with the decrease in eyestrain, has been found to increase learning by 10 per cent.

Various colors are being used for the board and for the crayon. There is a processed Masonite pressboard coated with a glossy smooth finish. On this various colors can be used. The crayon is no longer chalk, but a new composition. This is an advantage, for the annoyance of breathing chalk dust is obviated.

In constructing and placing the blackboard, size and height are of importance. Optimum results are not obtained if the board is too high or too low with reference to the floor. Basically the board is for the purpose of producing material which the entire class can easily see. If this is not so, it fails of its primary aim.

Uses of the Blackboard. As stated above, the blackboard is for the production of written or graphic materials that can be seen by the entire class. The blackboard has a number of undeniable advantages over any other visual device:

1. It is always available.
2. There is nothing to get out of order.
3. It is visible to the whole class.
4. New material can be presented immediately.
5. Material can be erased and something else written.
6. It is used by both teacher and pupils.

TEACHER USE. The teacher uses the blackboard for three main purposes, namely, for (a) teaching, (b) testing, and (c) assigning new work. For teaching the blackboard lends itself to:

1. The reproduction of original exercises or materials not found in the textbook. The latter phrase is important; it is not economical, in fact, it is wasteful for the teacher to fill the board with words, sentences, and paradigms that appear in print before the pupil. The teacher can, of course, in a developmental grammar lesson build up a tense or a series of forms like a synopsis and write all the forms on the board. In that case the weight will be on the teaching and learning aspects, especially the use of induction, deduction, and inference.

2. The writing of a new word or of a phrase or sentence for illustrative purposes. This is particularly valuable for teaching correct spelling, syllabication, intonation, and grammatical forms.

3. The presentation of material to be copied into notebooks. By writing it on the board the teacher avoids losing time through

lengthy dictation and prevents errors in spelling. Such material should be put on the board before the class has entered. It is preferable to keep such copying at a minimum; the major part of the period should be used for oral activities rather than for writing.

4. The teaching of new words. Word study forms an important part of most lessons and the blackboard is the most effective device for concentrating attention on the new vocabulary. Each new word can be elicited and written down by the teacher, or the list may already appear on the board, having been placed there by a reliable pupil. Each word is pronounced after the teacher, by the class and by individual pupils. After its meaning has been given, it is used in an original sentence.

5. Simple graphic representations. The easiest way of making clear what an unfamiliar object looks like is to put a simple outline drawing on the board. The teacher does not have to be a skilled artist to draw a simple outline of a Gothic window, a mansard, a poncho, or a gondola.

6. The giving of a test. In order to save time, the teacher will put the test questions on the board before the class enters.

7. The assigning of homework. The new assignment should be written in the foreign language, either by the teacher or by a pupil. It will be read aloud and translated by a pupil. New items will be rapidly checked, to see whether the class knows what is required.

PUPIL USE. The pupil will be called upon to use the blackboard for several types of writing activities, as follows:

1. The daily board exercise. Almost every lesson requires some work at the board by pupils. A common practice is to send a different row to the board every day. Each one is given a yellow slip of paper or a library card which contains a brief assignment or question based on the lesson. After each student has completed his work, he leaves the card on the board sill. A monitor takes up each card in turn and asks whether there are any errors in the board work. The card assignments should be short and significant. Each sentence or question should bring out some point of the lesson.

2. Homework. Another common practice is to have the homework assignment for the day put on the board by a number of pupils. To avoid loss of time and wrong impressions, fairly bright pupils should be chosen for this task. In this way the written work on the

board is likely to be correct. The class will make necessary corrections in the notebooks.

3. Practice in writing. After a pupil has replied to a question, he may be asked to go to the board and write his answer. This is especially good practice if a narrative is being reviewed and the questions follow in logical sequence. In that way the pupils will build up a composition.

4. Dictation. While the class is writing a dictation exercise, one student will write at the board. Preferably, he should write at a board at the rear of the room so that the class does not copy. When the exercise has been completed, the class faces about and compares its work with that on the board.

Types of Materials on the Blackboard. The blackboard can be used effectively for

1. Pictorial representations—drawings, sketches, diagrams, etc.
2. Outline maps.
3. Drawings of objects for pupils to label.
4. Vocabulary—new words, spelling, accent marks, elision, etc.
5. Sentences—illustrative.
6. Paradigms.
7. Development of a point in grammar.
8. Reviews.
9. Board work of the day, done by pupils from slips of paper.
10. New assignment.
11. Fill in exercises (these should be on board before class enters).
12. Test questions (these should be on board before class enters).

Formerly the blackboard was frequently used by the teacher for writing out "notes" to be copied by the pupils into notebooks. Although there was some pedagogic value in writing and copying, this is now considered time consuming and wasteful. Copying lengthy outlines during classtime is not considered economical. Any material that cannot be found in the textbook but is considered of sufficient importance should be duplicated and distributed to the pupils.

Optimum Use of the Blackboard. Since it is so readily taken for granted, the blackboard is not exploited thoroughly as a visual aid. This is particularly regrettable when one considers the importance of the eye in learning. To make the use of the blackboard more effective, the following factors should be considered:

1. The blackboard should never be overcrowded. A few important points, neatly written and in orderly arrangement, are far more effective than a mass of material. The board should be interesting and attractive, not dull and forbidding.

2. All writing on the board should be clear, neat, and orderly. In this regard the teacher should set an example. Illegible jottings, crude abbreviations, and inconsistencies in style are to be avoided. If manuscript writing or block lettering is used, it should not alternate with script—at least not in the same word or sentence! Anything that may be ambiguous, like the uncrossed *t* or the old-fashioned *r* that looks like *v* should be avoided. This is particularly important in a foreign language where the spelling is new to the pupil.

3. A definite routine should be established for the use of the board, so that no time is lost in going and coming, in looking for materials, etc. Equipment like chalk and erasers should be in their place before the class enters the room.

4. The use of colored chalk is effective for stressing key words, unusual spelling, verb endings, etc. For this purpose chrome yellow and pale green are the most effective.

5. The front boards should be given preference, so that there is as little necessity as possible for the class to turn in their seats. Boards in the rear should be used only for dictation or for material that is to remain on display for a number of days.

6. No errors should be left uncorrected, since the visual impression is a comparatively strong one.

7. Illumination is very important. The shades may have to be lowered to avoid sun-glare. On a dark day the lights should be switched on.

8. The material on the board should be visible to all pupils. This will demand not only clear and neat but fairly large script.

9. Blackboards should be cleaned after being used. Unrelated materials, previous assignments, etc. should be removed. It is not considered good to leave the work of a preceding class on the board, especially if it is material of another subject.

10. The efficient teacher will plan each day for the use of the blackboard.

Therapeutic Values for Pupils. Aside from its usefulness as a teaching device, the use of the blackboard offers several pleasurable aspects for the pupils. Among other things it

(a) provides a place where pupils can do written work which will be seen by their classmates,

(b) permits the pupils to show their skill in creative activities such as drawing, writing an original composition, etc.,

(c) affords the physical activity of going to the board and writing, which provides a moment of relaxation and recreation,

(d) calls upon the student to evaluate the written work of the pupil at the board, thus training the class in critical judgment.

The blackboard, then, is one of the most effective visual aids. As already indicated, however, it must be used skillfully to obtain optimum benefits. In great measure its importance is due to the fact that the sense of vision outweighs the other senses in most children. On the other hand—and this is significant in connection with the seating of the class—one fourth of our school children have defective vision.

The Flannel Board. The flannel board consists of a piece of flannel stretched over a piece of heavy cardboard or plywood. Any picture, clipping, or light flat object will adhere to the surface with a slight pressure of the hand. It obviates the use of thumbtacks or Scotch tape. The illustrative materials are easily attached; they are as easily removed.

The flannel board is widely used in the elementary grades for teaching color recognition, simple arithmetic, reading, word recognition, musical notation, and map work. With a little ingenuity complete diagrams and scenes can be built up, for any lightweight material will stick to the board.

In the foreign language classroom the board can be used effectively for the teaching of vocabulary. Cutouts are used to represent animals, articles of clothing, pieces of furniture, means of transportation, etc. They may be attached and detached by the pupil who will name the object as he manipulates it.

The flannel board has also been found useful for the teaching of a foreign language on television.

The Magneboard. A new device operating on the same principle as the flannel board is the magneboard. It consists of a smooth metal-like plastic rectangle which can be suspended on the wall or stood up on a table. Flat figurines and cutouts representing various objects can be slapped onto the board, which has magnetic properties. Since the surface is quite smooth, the cutouts can be moved around easily. They represent animals, different types of vehicles, buildings, etc. This device lends itself to the teaching of vocabulary in beginning classes.

DRAMATIZATION

PROBABLY NOTHING is superior to dramatization as an activity for practicing a foreign language. It is psychologically sound, for it connects the action with the spoken word. The actor has to think in the foreign language; there is no intermediate stage of translation. Speaking becomes practically automatic.

Dramatizing a scene or a dialogue is interesting and entertaining, for it adds a note of gaiety and liveliness to the classroom. It is interesting to the performer, since he is involved; it is entertaining to the class, since they are the spectators. It is educationally valuable, for it provides for much pupil participation and makes for spontaneity and self-expression.

Dramatization, in a simple way, may be engaged in practically from the first day of language instruction. "Bonjour, comment allez-vous? Très bien, et vous?" if spoken with some expression by two pupils before the class can become a lifelike situation.

From the memorized dialogue, the next step is spontaneous conversation, or at least conversation with variants. In the beginning the conversation may be guided and buttressed by words and expressions written on the board or supplied orally by the teacher.

Two factors essential to a convincing dramatization are the expressiveness and gestures of the actors and the use of props. Even the simplest objects and articles of clothing will add so much to the activity that they should not be omitted.

In the elementary school and with little children, these may consist of toys. Later they should be more like the real thing. A very useful and inexpensive device is the toy telephone. This can be used with equal effectiveness with fifth-grade pupils and with high-school students.

Typical conversations are:

> Inquiring as to health.
> Making a date to go to the movies.
> Discussing a movie that has been seen.

Calling the doctor.
Ordering groceries.

Each conversation should have a definite purpose and specific linguistic aims. The conversation with the doctor brings in the names of ailments; the talk with the grocer will be about foods. Of course, practically any subject may be discussed on the telephone.

The dramatization should not be too long. It should aim to provide for the participation of as many pupils as possible. Since in most daily activities only a limited number of persons are involved, it means that there will have to be a number of repetitions. This is no disadvantage; it may call forth a spirit of friendly rivalry. Each one will try to play his role better than his predecessor. The dramatic ability of the participants will be brought out.

Subjects for Dramatization. Subjects that lend themselves particularly well to dramatization are:

1. The family at home.
   Father reads paper; mother with pot or pan or broom; daughter with textbook, doing homework; son at telephone.
2. The family at table.
   Mother, wearing apron, serves food. Father and two or three children. Conversation while eating. (Table is teacher's desk covered with tablecloth.)
3. Visit of the doctor.
   Doctor has toy stethoscope. Son ill; lies down or reclines on two chairs. Pillow; tumbler. Mother solicitous. Conversation about ailments.
4. Visit to doctor or dentist.
   Nurse, with cap. Doctor with stethoscope and reflector. Nurse gets information about name, address, age, etc. Doctor prescribes.
5. Shopping.
   Storekeeper; customers, in succession. Conversation provides for many variations in names of materials, colors, sizes, prices, etc. Props: stockings, hats, shoes, boxes, etc. Types of stores:
   (a) hats
   (b) shoes
   (c) men's wear
   (d) dresses
   (e) toys (with children)
   (f) stationery
   (g) department store

(h) grocery
(i) fruit stand.

6. Travel.

Tourist, hat on, carries suitcase:
(a) at travel agent's (maps, folders)
(b) buying rail, bus, or air ticket
(c) on the boat (captain with cap)
(d) on the train (conductor with cap)
(e) at customs (officer with cap)
(f) getting information from foreign policeman.

7. Barbershop.

Barber, apron, toy razor or clipper or shears.

8. Setting the table.

Mother, apron; gives orders to children. Dishes.

9. In the kitchen.

Mother prepares meal. Pot, pan, apron.

10. Restaurant scene.

A number of guests at table. Waiter. Tablecloth, dishes, menu, towel.

ILLUSTRATIVE LESSONS

Dramatized Fairy Tale

(French)

SLEEPING BEAUTY

(This lesson was planned and carried out by Mrs. Adele Fugazy of P.S. 196, Queens, New York.)

Eight of the children in this fifth-grade class who showed evidence of dramatic ability were chosen for the eight leading parts in the play *Cinderella*. These parts were: the king, the queen, the princesses, the good fairy, the witch, the cook, the prince, and his friend. The rest of the class played the parts of courtiers who made chorus responses at various points in the action. Also, they sang a number of French songs to add a musical touch to the performance. These were: "Sur le pont d'Avignon," "Au clair de la lune," and "Savez-vous planter les choux?"

The costumes of the leading characters were designed by various children, based upon pictures that the teacher provided. They were made in co-operation with the Home Economics department of the school.

After the lines had been learned and the play rehearsed in class, it was produced on the stage of the auditorium. The acting was done so well that it could be followed even by children who had had no French. However, to help them understand better, each character introduced himself at the beginning of the play and a commentator would step in occasionally with a very brief comment in English. ("Here comes the bad witch—and is she bad!")

Also, each scene was announced before it was put on.

The script, which employed the simplest expressions and commonest words and still was lively, interesting, and humorous was as follows:

(Taken from *Petites Conversations* by Julian Harris and Hélène Monod-Cassidy, University of Wisconsin Press, pp. 58–61.)

La Belle au Bois Dormant

Scene I

(No scenery used; simply four chairs for king, queen, and princesses.)

MASTER OF CEREMONIES: We are going to play *The Sleeping Beauty* for you.

CHILD: En français, *La Belle au bois dormant*.

KING: *(comes in wearing a high crown)* Je suis le roi. *(Bows and sits down on throne.)*

QUEEN: *(comes in wearing smaller crown; bows and sits next to king)* Je suis la reine.

PRINCESS SISTER: *(comes in, bows; wears silver paper crown)* Je suis la petite sœur.

PRINCESS: *(comes in and bows; wears gold paper crown; sits next to king)* Je suis la princesse.

KING: *(hands princess a gift)* Bonjour, princesse, bonne fête.

QUEEN: *(hands princess a gift also)* Bonjour, princesse, bonne fête.

PRINCESS: Bonjour, mon père; bonjour, ma mère. Merci beaucoup. J'ai quinze ans aujourd'hui!

SISTER: *(claps her hands; gives her small present)* Bonne fête. Vous avez quinze ans. Vous êtes jolie.

KING: Riche!

QUEEN: Bonne!

COOK: *(comes in wearing tall chef's hat)* Princesse, que voulez-vous comme dessert?

PRINCESS: *(gestures with hands)* Un gâteau à la crème.

SISTER: Et de la glâce au chocolat!

COOK: Tout de suite, mesdemoiselles. *(Exit)*

M.C.: *(with tragic voice, from the side)* Here comes the wicked fairy!

2 6

WICKED FAIRY: (wears a tall hat of black paper) Bonjour, princesse.

PRINCESS: (shyly) Bonjour, madame.

KING: (scared) Que voulez-vous, madame?

WICKED FAIRY: (laughs sardonically) Voilà un cadeau pour la princesse. (Hands her a spindle; stick with wound yarn.) Bonne fête, mon enfant!

QUEEN: Princesse, princesse, montrez-moi ce cadeau. J'ai peur!

PRINCESS: Mais non, ma mère. Regardez, c'est un joli cadeau, n'est-ce pas?

WICKED FAIRY: (laughs) Très, très joli!

PRINCESS: Merci beaucoup, madame. (She pricks herself.) Ah, ah, ah! (Falls to floor with one arm on chair, head on arm.)

KING: Gardes, gardes, vite! (Six or eight guards come in, lift the princess and put her on a bed. A folded blanket is at her side.)

WICKED FAIRY: (Laughs) Ah, ah, ah, regardez ma jolie princesse!

QUEEN: (weeps) Ma fille, ma petite fille!

KING: (weeps) Ma fille, ma princesse!

SISTER: (weeps) Ma sœur, ma sœur!

M.C.: (from side, with sigh of relief) Here comes the good fairy.

GOOD FAIRY: (star on forehead, white dress; bows) Je suis la bonne fée.

QUEEN: Ah, madame, regardez ma pauvre fille.

KING: Ma fille est malade.

GOOD FAIRY: Princesse, vous allez dormir cent ans.

WICKED FAIRY: Ah, ah, ah, cent ans!

ALL: Au revoir, princesse, au revoir; dormez bien. (They all sing softly "La Belle au bois dormant." All leave as they sing the last line.)

(Curtain)

Scene II

(Same scene. Princess asleep. Guards asleep on their feet around throne.)

M.C.: (comes in) Here come Prince Charming and his friend.

PRINCE: (wears a sword and small crown) Je suis le Prince Charmant (gestures) et voilà le château.

FRIEND: (wears sword but no crown) Où est la princesse?

PRINCE: Oh, regarde, voilà la princesse.

FRIEND: Elle est très jolie.

PRINCE: Oui, elle est très jolie. Elle dort.

FRIEND: Embrassez-la, mon prince.

PRINCE: (kisses her) Princesse!

PRINCESS: (waking) Ah! Où est ma mère? Est-ce que mon père est ici?

PRINCE: Je suis le Prince Charmant. Je vous aime.

GOOD FAIRY: *(comes in softly)* Princesse, levez-vous. Voilà votre prince.

PRINCESS: *(with curtsy)* Merci beaucoup, madame. *(Shyly)* Bonjour, prince.

PRINCE: *(on his knees; kisses her hand)* Princesse! *(Leads her to throne.)*

COOK: *(appears with a tray of cakes and candies)* Voilà des gâteaux et des bonbons. Princesse, voulez-vous des bonbons?

PRINCESS: Avec plaisir. *(Shyly)* Prince, voulez-vous des bonbons? *(Prince takes some.)*

(All come upon the stage and shout: Vive le prince! Vive la princesse!*)*

(All sing "La Belle au bois dormant" in a gay manner.)

KING: Chantons et dansons maintenant.

Sur le pont d'Avignon *(Eight pupils dance while others sing.)*

Savez-vous planter les choux? *(One pupil explains in English.)*

(All line up across the stage and sing. One third act "avec le nez," next third act "avec les pieds," last third "avec les mains.") Au claire de la lune.

(Curtain)

Use of Marionettes

(French)

CINDERELLA

(This lesson was planned and carried out by Mrs. Gertrude Pucie of P.S. 196, Queens, New York.)

All the pupils in the fourth-grade class taught by the teacher participated in the project, which resulted in a performance in the school auditorium.

About fifteen pupils, who had ability in drawing, volunteered to prepare slides to illustrate the chief episodes in the French fairy tale. Although the slides, as it turned out, were somewhat lacking in uniformity of style and treatment, they were extremely interesting because each pupil had interpreted the characters according to his own imagination. Since the story of Cinderella, however, is generally known, this caused no difficulty.

In class each child gave a brief description, orally, of the scene on his slide. These statements were prepared with the help of the teacher. In the auditorium, for the sake of the pupils present who had not had any French, the descriptions were given in English.

The marionettes were prepared by a group of other pupils. The figures represented Cinderella, the two sisters, the fairy godmother, two courtiers, and the prince. The glass slipper, somewhat larger than the puppet's foot, also was represented.

The pupils who made the marionettes were assigned to manipulate them. A curtain was spread over the front of a table to cover it completely. Another curtain, suspended from the top, extended six inches beyond the table, so as to allow space for the operation of the marionettes.

For the speaking parts a number of pupils said the parts of the various marionettes in French. In the auditorium they stood at either end of the platform. This arrangement, of course, can be varied by having the marionette players recite the parts. The two obvious difficulties would be the strain on the pupil who has to operate the marionette and speak the part in the foreign language, and the possibility that the voice might not be heard from behind the curtain.

The script for the marionette show was as follows:

(Based upon "Cendrillon" in *Lire et Apprendre*, Ungar Publishlishing Co., New York)

(Used with puppets, Fourth Grade)

Puppets

(French)

CENDRILLON

Scene I

La chambre de Juliette et de Françoise

JULIETTE: Cendrillon!

CENDRILLON: Me voici.

JULIETTE: Je veux mes pantoufles.

FRANÇOISE: Je veux ma robe. Vite! *(Cendrillon court de l'une à l'autre.)*

JULIETTE: Où est la robe? Dépêche-toi.

CENDRILLON: Oh, je veux aller au bal aussi.

FRANÇOISE: Non, non, Cendrillon.

CENDRILLON: Qu'elles sont méchantes! Je suis triste.

(Rideau)

Scene II

Cendrillon est au jardin. Elle est assise près d'un arbre. Elle pleure.

LA FÉE: Cendrillon!

CENDRILLON: Qui êtes-vous?

LA FÉE: Je suis votre marraine. Je vous aime bien. Vous voulez aller au bal, n'est-ce pas? Voici une robe.

CENDRILLON: Ah, que vous êtes bonne! Que je suis heureuse! La robe, elle est belle!

LA FÉE: Et les pantoufles.

CENDRILLON: Qu'elles sont mignonnes! Elles sont tout en cristal.

LA FÉE: Et vos bas.

CENDRILLON: Qu'ils sont beaux!

LA FÉE: Habillez-vous vite!

CENDRILLON: Maintenant je suis belle comme mes sœurs. Merci, ma bonne marraine.

LA FÉE: Voici un carosse. Rentrez à minuit, Cendrillon! N'oubliez pas, à minuit.

CENDRILLON: Ma bonne marraine, je vous remercie de tout mon cœur. Je suis bien contente.

(Rideau)

Scene III

La grande salle du château royal. Le prince, Cendrillon, Juliette, Françoise, et beaucoup d'invités.

FRANÇOISE: Qui est cette belle dame qui danse avec le prince?

JULIETTE: Je ne la connais pas. Le prince danse toujours avec elle.

LE PRINCE: Comment vous appelez-vous? Dites-le-moi. Vous êtes très belle, la plus belle de toutes les jeunes filles. Je vous adore. *(En ce moment on entend sonner minuit.)*

CENDRILLON: Oh . . . il est minuit . . . il faut que je parte. *(Elle quitte le prince. En courant elle perd une de ses pantoufles. Le prince la ramasse.)*

LE PRINCE: Une pantoufle.

(Rideau)

Scene IV

Juliette et Françoise sont au salon. Le prince entre avec la petite pantoufle à la main.

LE PRINCE: Permettez-moi de vous essayer cette pantoufle.

JULIETTE: *(l'essaye)* Oh, elle est trop petite.

FRANÇOISE: *(l' essaye)* Oh . . . Oh . . . que ça fait mal!

LE PRINCE: N'avez-vous pas une autre sœur?

JULIETTE: Si, elle est à la cuisine.

LE PRINCE: Appelez votre sœur, s'il vous plaît. Je veux la voir.

FRANÇOISE: *(ouvre la porte)* Cendrillon! *(Elle entre.)*

LE PRINCE: Voulez-vous essayer cette pantoufle?

CENDRILLON: Volontiers.

30

LE PRINCE: Ah . . . c'est vous. Vous êtes la belle princesse du bal. Je suis content. Voulez-vous être ma femme?

CENDRILLON: *(joyeuse)* Je veux bien, car je vous aime de tout mon cœur.

(Rideau)

A la fin tous chantent "Dites-moi." Cendrillon et le prince dansent.

Dramatization

(German)

BEIM DOKTOR

A boy plays the role of the doctor; a girl is the nurse. A succession of pupils come in as patients. The doctor's office is at the teacher's desk.

The doctor should wear a reflector—made of a small mirror or a circular piece of tin attached to a band of cloth—around his forehead. A small short kitchen sprayer hose will serve as a stethoscope. The nurse will wear a white nurse's cap.

The nurse greets each patient as he enters. The doctor asks questions about the patient's ailments and prescribes a remedy.

The conversation is as follows:

> NURSE: Guten Tag.
> PATIENT: Guten Tag.
> N: Was wünschen Sie, mein Herr?
> P: Ich möchte den Doktor sprechen.
> N: Gut. Wie heissen Sie?
> P: Carl Miller. *(Nurse writes on a pad.)*
> N: Und wie ist Ihre Adresse?
> P: 108 Park Avenue.
> N: Wie alt sind Sie?
> P: Zweiunddreissig.
> N: Sind Sie schon mal hier gewesen?
> P: Nein.
> N: Was ist Ihr Beruf?
> P: Ich bin Zimmermann.

This conversation permits the use of a number of variant answers with reference to name, address, age, vocation, etc.

The nurse steps aside: the doctor steps forward. He looks at the card.

> D: Guten Tag, Herr Miller.
> P: Guten Tag, Herr Doktor.

D: Bitte setzen Sie sich.

P: Danke. *(sits down.)*

D: Was fehlt Ihnen?

P: Ich habe Kopfschmerzen.

D: Jeden Tag?

P: Jeden Morgen.

D: Wie ist Ihr Appetit?

P: Nicht so gut.

D: Werden Sie leicht müde?

P: Ja.

D: Stecken Sie Ihre Zunge heraus, bitte.

P: *(Sticks tongue out.)*

D: Gut. Atmen Sie ein. *(Uses stethoscope.)*

P: *(Inhales.)*

D: Noch einmal!

P: *(Inhales.)*

D: Gut. Sie sind blutarm. Ich gebe Ihnen etwas dafür. Es ist nicht ernst. Hier ist das Rezept. Nehmen Sie jeden Abend einen Teelöffel davon.

P: Danke, Herr Doktor.

D: Auf Wiedersehen, Herr Miller.

Several different ways of teaching the same subject:

Names of Dishes

(Spanish)

A. WITH PICTURES

Using mounted pictures or simple outline drawings of different dishes, the teacher names each object as she shows the picture. The class repeats in concert; pupils repeat individually.

As each dish is named, the Spanish word is written on the blackboard. The vocabulary will be limited to the following words:

taza	cuchillo	mantel
platillo	tenedor	servilleta
vaso	cuchara	

The following adjectives may be added

frío	limpio
caluroso	sucio

The verb *poner* will be reviewed and used with the meaning to set, to place *(poner la mesa)*.

Conversation on the basis of the pictures can be built up as follows:

> ¿De qué color es la taza?
> ¿Qué hay en la taza?
> ¿Qué hay en el plato?
> ¿Qué usamos para cortar la carne?
> ¿Qué usamos para tomar la sopa?
> ¿Qué hay a la derecha del plato?
> ¿Qué hay a la izquierda del plato?
> Esta cuchara no está limpia; está sucia.

B. WITH PROPS

A set of cheap china or plastic dishes has been placed on the window sill or on a cabinet, in preparation for an activity which may be called "Setting the Table" (*"Poniendo la mesa"*). The first pupil who is called on goes to the table, or the teacher's desk, and places a cloth on it, saying, "Pongo el mantel en la mesa." Other pupils follow and each one places a dish on the table, describing his action as he performs it.

> Pongo una taza en la mesa.
> Pongo un plato en la mesa.
> Pongo un vaso en la mesa.

Variety can be introduced by having the teacher or a pupil give the command, "Ponga Vd. un cuchillo en la mesa." Or, another pupil may describe the action in the third person: "El pone un vaso en la mesa."

Another variation is possible by assuming that the table is being set for a family with a given number of persons.

> Pongo un plato en la mesa. Es grande porque es para papá. El come mucho.
> Pongo un vaso en la mesa. Es grande porque es para tío Juan. El bebe mucho.
> Pongo un plato. Es pequeño porque es para Anita. Ella es pequeña. No come mucho.

C. WITH DRAWINGS ON THE BOARD

The teacher draws a large rectangle on the board to resemble a table. Pupils are called upon, or get up, in sequence and go up to the board. Each one takes the chalk and draws a dish within the rectangle, saying

> Pongo una taza en la mesa, etc.

When a given number of covers have been completed—say six—the last pupil can announce: "La mesa está puesta."

A variation that can be introduced is to have each pupil label in Spanish the dish he has drawn.

In the same lesson, or in the next one, the activity can be elaborated by adding foods to the dishes. These might include

café	carne	sopa
té	patatas	pescado
leche	guisantes	queso
agua	pan	fruta
vino	mantequilla	

Each pupil puts something into a cup or onto a plate, following the procedure described above. A pupil may be assigned to each place. He may comment, as he is served: "Bastante" or "Más, por favor." "Gracias."

The last pupils will announce, "La comida está servida."

Dramatization

(French)

AU RESTAURANT

A very interesting and useful activity for teaching the names of foods and dishes is the restaurant scene. A good deal of foreign culture may be introduced, too. It is a favorite for the French assembly program but can be used quite as effectively, for instruction, in the classroom. To make it colorful and to give it an air of verisimilitude, a few props should be used. With a little skill a textbook dialogue can be transformed into a fascinating little dramatization.

Phonograph plays French vocal or instrumental record. Teacher's desk is covered with a tablecloth. Some dishes are there. Four chairs are placed near the desk.

Four students, two boys and two girls, approach the desk and enter into a conversation about as follows:

—Ah, voilà, un bon restaurant!
—Oui, je l'aime beaucoup.
—Asseyons-nous près de la fenêtre.
—Oui.
Waiter *(student with towel)* enters.
—Bonjour, messieurs, mesdames. Qu'est ce que je peux vous servir?
—Donnez-nous la carte, s'il vous plaît.
—La voici, monsieur. *(Hands it to him.)*

34

—Que recommandez-vous aujourd'hui?
—La côtelette de veau, monsieur.
—Bon. Donnez-m'en, si'l vous plaît.
—Moi, je désire de la soupe à l'oignon.
—Et moi, de la bouillabaisse.
—Très bien, madame. *(Waiter goes.)*
—J'ai faim.
—Moi aussi.
—Voilà le garçon! *(Waiter serves.)*
—Ah, que j'aime cela. *(Eats.)*
(Conversation continues)
—Garçon, l'addition, s'il vous plaît.
—La voilà, monsieur. *(Guest hands him money.)*
—Merci bien. Au revoir, messieurs, mesdames.
—Au revoir!

The conversation during the meal can be expanded, depending upon the imagination, resourcefulness, and vocabulary of the pupils.

Several pairs of students should be able to enact the scene within one period.

FLAT MATERIALS

FOR EVERYDAY USE there are a number of very simple, inexpensive, and effective visual materials that can easily be made by the teacher herself. These include flash cards, pronunciation charts, and a clock dial.

Flash Cards. The flash card is a piece of oak tag or cardboard about 18 x 6 inches on which appears a word, a sentence, or a simple outline drawing. The lettering should be large, neat, and clear so that it can be seen from the rear of the room. Capital letters are preferred. Script should not be used since it is difficult to read at a distance.

Both sides of the card can be used, especially for teaching vocabulary. The foreign word will be on one side, the translation on the other. Thus a double drill exercise can be given. First, the English word is displayed and the foreign equivalent is elicited; then the foreign word is shown and its English meaning is given.

Flash Card Exercises. What types of exercises may be given by means of flash cards? The ingenious teacher will find that a great variety of linguistic forms can be practiced with this simple device. For example:

1. Vocabulary. (English word on one side, foreign word on reverse side)
2. Verb forms.
     (a) Completion. (Nous finis . . .)
     (b) Insertion of pronoun. (Parles- . . . ?)
     (c) Translation to foreign language. (We were going.)
     (d) Translation into English. (Il fit)
3. Adjectives.
     (a) Completion. (lecciones fácil . . .)
     (b) Insertion of suitable adjective. (Trabaja mucho; es . . .)
     (c) Opposites. (No es pobre, es . . .)
     (d) Synonyms. (hermoso)
4. Nouns
     (a) Plural. (francés . . .)
     (b) Feminine. (mejor, . . .)
     (c) Pair. (buey, . . .)
     (d) Function. (Vemos con . . .)
5. Prepositions.
     (a) Insertion. (Consiste . . . 5 personas.)
     (b) Translation. (I think of her.)
6. Adverbs.
     (a) Formation from adjective. (rápido)
     (b) Comparative and superlative. (bueno)

Brevity, is of course, the soul of the flash card. Five words would seem to be the limit, otherwise a second line is needed, which is not desirable.

Pictures, that is, very simple outline sketches, can be used too. Suggested subjects are the names of

1. Animals.
2. Fruits.
3. Dishes.
4. Pieces of furniture.
5. Articles of clothing.
6. Means of transportation.
7. Members of the family.

The exercise may be varied from mere identification to a descriptive sentence or two.

La madre.
La madre ocupada.
La madre prepara las comidas.
El perro.
El perro pequeño.
El perro es pequeño. Se llama Toto, piensa en su almuerzo. Tiene hambre.

The cards can be displayed by the teacher or by a student. The latter is preferable, since it makes for pupil participation.

The sets of cards should be filed away under given categories. They will be found very useful for review, for drill, and as a warming-up exercise at the beginning of the period.

Still Pictures

The great difference between a motion picture and a still picture is that the former shows life in action whereas the latter merely suggests action. The motion picture, then, is useful primarily for showing continuous action, processions, activities, and processes. In many instances, however, it is far more effective to concentrate on the scene and to eliminate motion. This is particularly true of scenery, buildings, architectural and other detail, costumes, etc.

It is important for the teacher to imagine in advance how the pupils will interpret the picture. The same illustration may mean different things to different people, depending upon their racial and religious background, their educational status, their emotional reactions, and the acuity of their vision. A picture does not necessarily make a universal appeal; its interpretation is conditioned by group and individual reactions.

Reading has been defined as "getting the meaning from the printed page." The same definition may be applied to the interpretation of a picture; it, too, is read. The child recognizes the various elements of a pictorial representation on the basis of his knowledge and his past experience. If a picture shows something entirely new or strange, he may be completely at a loss.

When a child is asked, "What do you see in this picture?" he will begin to enumerate objects and persons he recognizes. The next question may be, "What do you think is happening?" or "What are they doing?" At this point the child is called upon to use his imagination. He has been enumerating or describing; now he is to fill out, to elaborate. This is a matter of inference.

Visual Materials and Techniques / 37

It is obvious that the pupil—especially the very young child—must be prepared and guided by the teacher. He must be told what to look for or he may miss the significant elements in the picture.

Kinds of Pictures

The term "picture" includes every type of pictorial representation. The simpler kind consists of illustrations clipped from books, magazines, and newspapers, e.g., photographs, lithographs, color prints, line drawings, halftones, etc. These can easily be mounted and filed with appropriate labels.

In fact, for the teaching of culture, a rather complete file of such illustrative materials should be maintained. In the high school the chairman will have such a file in his office and will lend the materials to his teachers as needed.

A larger and usually more colorful type of illustration is the poster. Because of its size, it is difficult to handle. In most cases it occupies a permanent place on the wall. If the posters on display in the classroom have been selected with care, they will be referred to whenever the occasion arises. They should be of value not only from the point of view of decoration but also as pedagogic material.

A smaller type of pictorial representation that can be used very effectively in the teaching of civilization is the picture postcard. The teacher may have built up a rich collection on the basis of her travels abroad. They can easily be filed under appropriate categories. The best way to use them is to pass them around the class for individual inspection.

For use in front of the class, the picture card is much too small. For group attention only the poster and the picture should be used. The latter should be large and clear enough so that it can be seen from the back of the room. It is also well to mount it so that it remains flat. If it is displayed on the wall, it ought to be labeled in clear type.

HOW TO USE PICTURES. One of the basic principles to observe in the use of pictures is that a limited number of pertinent and well-selected pictures is far preferable to a multitude of heterogeneous, ill-assorted illustrations.

For the effective use of pictorial materials the following suggestions are made:

1. Preparation. In view of the fact that we are surrounded by pictures, posters, billboards, and signs of a high technical quality and that the magazines present a plethora of beautiful illustrations in color, the mere presentation of a picture in the classroom will not arouse immediate and profound interest. The class must be put into a receptive mood; the showing of the picture must be motivated. Furthermore, the pupils must be told what to observe and what to remember.

2. Presentation. Powers of observation, like those of listening, are not inborn; they must be trained. Many people are not fully aware of the significance of what they see or hear. Very few pictures are self-explanatory. The teacher is there to point out the important factors, to clarify, to stress and emphasize, to explain. This is important because children's experiences are inadequate and we all interpret what we see and hear in the light of our past experience.

3. Application. The information obtained should be applied. This can be done in a number of ways. If the picture is used for purely linguistic aims, the new words and phrases should be used in original sentences, in dictation, and in short compositions. If it is a lesson in culture, the pupils may be inspired to do further reading and research, and to report on the subject.

SIZE OF PICTURE. A picture shown to the class must, of course, be fairly large, so that it can be seen by everyone. The colored covers of the larger magazines like *Life, Look,* the *Saturday Evening Post,* and the *Ladies Home Journal,* which are about 11 x 15 inches, lend themselves to this purpose. The many fine illustrations found in the *National Geographic* are too small for group showing.

Smaller pictures, illustrations, clippings, and postcards can be used for individual inspection. In this connection the suggestion is made that such material not be sent around the room while the teacher is talking; that is definitely distracting. It is much better to have this done while there is silence; the teacher may circulate and comment to groups of students while they are looking at the material.

Some of the smaller items may be used later for display on the bulletin board. If they are to be used for group inspection, the teacher should show them by means of the opaque projector.

Projection of Pictures. For ordinary purposes and to save time it is best to use large mounted pictures or line drawings. However, a vast amount of material is in color and of so intricate a nature that it would be futile to try to reproduce it by copying. This is particularly true of photographs of persons, color reproductions of famous paintings, and maps. These should be taken as they are and projected onto a screen.

The Opaque Projector. The most effective machine for doing this is the opaque projector. It can project onto a screen or a wall anything printed, painted, or drawn. It will take photographs, halftones, line drawings, illustrations, handwritten notes, charts, sketches, and maps. The material need not even be mounted; a book or magazine can be put into the projector. In fact, it will even project flat objects such as stamps, coins, handkerchiefs, medals, etc. Since the object is projected by means of reflected light, the light has to be much stronger than in the case of a film projector. The room must be darker.

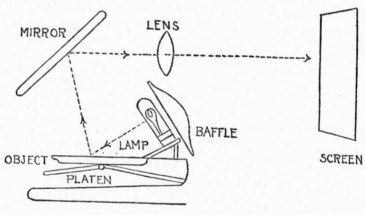

HOW THE OPAQUE PROJECTOR WORKS

The controls consist of the lamp switch, which also turns on the power; the platen handle—the crank for the conveyer belt; and, on some models, an illuminated pointer. In setting up the projector, the distance from the screen must be watched, so that a clear image results. Also, the room must be quite dark.

There is a small door on one side of the machine which can be opened. The book, magazine, or picture to be projected is placed on the "floor" of the machine. Light is furnished by a 500-watt bulb. By a series of mirrors the object placed on the floor inside the machine is reflected through the lens in front and can be directed toward a screen across the room. Some opaque projectors accommodate materials no larger than 4 x 4 inches; others have an opening large enough for 6 x 6 inches. The maximum is usually 10 x 10 inches.

SPECIAL USES OF THE OPAQUE PROJECTOR. One special use of the opaque projector is in the correction of compositions or other written work. The teacher may take an uncorrected composition or a homework paper and insert it in the machine. It is thus made visible to the entire class for group correction, directed reading, or critical evaluation. Much painful copying on the blackboard can be saved in this way. The clarity also is greater.

If, on the other hand, the teacher has already made the corrections and feels that they are of common interest to the class, the corrected composition can be flashed on the screen for the purpose of drill, oral practice, or comment.

Sight reading of materials printed abroad is valuable. Foreign language texts are not, however, always available in quantity. By using the opaque projector a single copy of a newspaper or a page from a textbook becomes available for group study. The saving in mimeographing is considerable. Moreover, the mimeographed sheet does not reproduce the exact appearance of the foreign publication and thus a significant characteristic is lost. The front page of *Paris Soir* looks quite different from the front page of the *New York Times*. The opaque projector, however, presents an exact reproduction and retains everything essential. A lesson with a newspaper will then become more than a mere exercise in reading. It will involve appreciation of journalistic style, newspaper arrangement, differences in treatment of news, etc. In other words, the cultural as well as the linguistic will be considered.

Since the opaque projector works well only in a completely darkened room, the lesson must be so planned that only oral activities are involved. Writing, for instance, would require light. This is also a reason for using the projector at the beginning of the period.

The teacher may show a picture of a scene in the foreign country. The picture would remain on the screen for five minutes, during which time the teacher would point out what was to be noted. Questions would be asked and the pupils would reply and comment. A series of pictures may be used. Then the normal illumination of the room would be restored and the discussion of the subject could continue. Perhaps reading of related material in the book would follow. Finally, a dictation exercise in the foreign language, based on the pictures, would end the lesson.

ADVANTAGES OF THE OPAQUE PROJECTOR. The opaque projector is a very useful teaching device. It is surprising that it has not been used more. Its special advantages are:

1. It is portable.
2. It is inexpensive.
3. There are no movable parts to get out of order.
4. It is equally useful on all levels; it can be used as effectively in a college class as in the kindergarten.
5. It covers the widest possible range and will project any non-transparent material. Anything can be shown from a color reproduction of the "Mona Lisa" to a page from the morning newspaper.
6. Small objects and pictures, which would ordinarily have to be passed around the class, can be used for group instruction.

Examples of Projectable Materials. The range of materials that the opaque projector will accommodate is practically unlimited. Here follow some examples:

1. Colored reproductions of famous paintings clipped from books or magazines, or mounted on cardboard.
2. Postcards, picture cards.
3. Bills of fare.
4. Stamps, coins, railway tickets, checks, etc.
5. Small maps in books.
6. Photographs of eminent men and women, in books, in magazines.
7. Pages from newspapers in the foreign language.
8. Diagrams showing succession of kings, organization of governments, school systems, etc.
9. Past examination questions, for review.
10. Flags of various countries.
11. Words of a song.
12. Costume plates.

A glance at the above will show immediately how useful the opaque projector is for the presentation of cultural illustrative material. In each instance, however, the picture can be used as the basis of discussion or conversation in the foreign language. The projector can be used, too, to throw an enlarged version of a map or diagram on the blackboard for the purpose of tracing it.

Advantages of Projection. The teacher may question the projecting of pictures in view of the time entailed in setting up the machine, darkening the room, and getting the material together. However, the projected picture is such an effective teaching device that it will repay all the trouble taken.

Basically, a socialized recitation is established. The entire class looks at the same thing at the same time. It is a shared experience. Furthermore, any individual pupil can ask questions or make comments during the projection.

Darkening the room and projecting pictures is a desirable variation of routine. The unusualness of the procedure and its dramatic qualities concentrate attention on the picture. Interest is aroused, there are pleasurable emotional reactions. A foreign atmosphere is easily created. An optimum learning situation is established.

Slides

KINDS OF SLIDES. Slides come in two sizes, 2 x 2 inches or $3\frac{1}{4}$ x 4 inches. The teacher can make his own slides, but this is really not necessary when such excellent professional material is available. Slides are best used for teaching cultural matters, that is, for showing the pupil what life is like in the foreign country. If the teacher has traveled and has taken pictures himself, the showing of such slides adds to the interest, for personal reminiscences may be included.

The talk may be given in English or, slowly and simply, in the foreign language. New and difficult expressions may be given in translation. A judicious combination of the foreign language and English will prove interesting and effective.

A useful procedure is to have pupils prepare the lecture. Each one gets a slide or several slides to study. A brief paragraph is written out for each slide. The teacher goes over the notes, makes corrections, and hears the pupil give his talk. On the day of the lesson each pupil proceeds to speak as his slide or slides appear on the screen.

USEFULNESS OF THE SLIDE. The slide possesses these advantages:

1. It lends itself to group appeal.
2. It focuses the attention of the class.
3. It stimulates thought on the part of the pupils.
4. It may be held any length of time and can readily be repeated.
5. It can be correlated with any part of the curriculum.

Government offices and foreign language aid bureaus maintain sets of slides on the geography of the country, as well as on famous buildings, paintings, and sculpture. Usually a manuscript accompanies the set of slides. Even if this is not particularly good, it can be used as a source of information.

ADVANTAGES. The glass slide is one of the most useful of visual aids. Actually it is the basis of all projection, for a motion picture is merely a succession of still pictures in a given sequence.

Motion, however, is not required at all times. In the case of landscapes, buildings, street scenes, and portraits motion is entirely irrelevant. The particular advantages of the glass slide projector are:

1. It is easy to operate.
2. It is relatively inexpensive.
3. It lends itself to a variety of uses.
4. It can be used on all school levels.
5. It produces a brilliantly illuminated image even if the room is only partially darkened. In fact, the room need not be darkened at all if a short focal lens is used.
6. Almost any kind of screen is adequate.
7. The slides may be examined at length. There is plenty of time for detailed observation, analysis, questions, and discussion.

LIMITATIONS. However, as in the case of other audio-visual media, there are certain disadvantages in the use of the slide. Motion and action are, of course, lost. Also, the slide does not portray anything in the third dimension. That is where the stereograph is far more effective; it gives a realistic impression of spatial depth. Finally, slides are heavy and bulky and are easily broken.

CRITERIA. In selecting slides observe the following criteria:

1. Authenticity. Is the picture a good one? Is it accurate?
2. Photography. Is the photography technically perfect?
3. Quality. Is the slide free of blemishes, scratches, smudges? Is it bound? Does it have a thumb mark? Does it have a caption?

The Filmstrip

The filmstrip is the simplest kind of projected still picture in a sequence. It consists of a series of illustrations printed on 35-mm. film. The pictures may be of the single frame type, $\frac{3}{4}$ x 1 inches, or double frame, $1\frac{1}{2}$ x 1 inches. The single frame strip is that which is used most commonly. It is also possible to mount 2 x 2-inch frames. The filmstrip may be accompanied by sound; it is then known as a slidefilm. This will be described later; here we are confining our selves to the visual aspect.

ADVANTAGES. For certain purposes the filmstrip has decided advantages in the classroom over the ordinary film and even over the motion picture. The filmstrip

1. Retains unity.
2. Is enriched and clarified by accompanying comments and discussion.
3. Can be moved forward or backward with ease.
4. Is simple to operate.
5. Is economical. (A roll of 25–75 pictures can be secured for less then 10 cents a picture.)
6. Is easy to handle—a strip weighs less than an ounce and can be held in the palm of the hand.

For motion, activity, and continuity of action the motion picture is preferable. For the showing of landscapes, scenes, persons, objects, and buildings the still picture is more effective. In the motion picture these lose their sense of stability; an unnecessary and disturbing factor of motion is introduced.

USE OF FILMSTRIP. The filmstrip is a very useful teaching device. To secure greatest effectiveness, the following suggestions should be observed:

1. The teacher will preview the film so as to judge its suitability and its place in the lesson.

2. The film should be introduced with proper motivation, so that the pupils know what to expect and what to look for.
3. The teacher need not feel obliged to confine himself to the captions or to the manual. The presentation of the material should be free and spontaneous.
4. Pupils should be encouraged to comment freely.
5. The strip should be shown at the beginning of the lesson, so that there will be time for discussion and application.
6. The teacher should have guiding questions ready before the showing of the film. Oral and written activities may follow the showing.

QUALITY OF THE FILMSTRIP. In selecting filmstrips, the following criteria may be observed:

1. Is the subject matter appropriate?
2. Are the pictures sequential?
3. Is the vocabulary of the right level?
4. Are the pictures interesting?
5. Are they clear?
6. Do they lend themselves to expanded oral discussion?

The Filmstrip Projector. The filmstrip projector is so simple to handle, that a pupil can take care of it.

The controls consist of the lamp switch, the blower switch, and the transport knob. There are different types of projectors. Some are adapted to 2 x 2-inch slides as well as filmstrips.

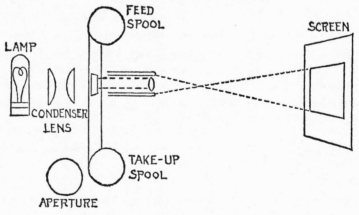

HOW THE FILMSTRIP PROJECTOR WORKS

The important thing is to have the machine set up properly and checked before the showing of the filmstrip.

LESSON WITH FILMSTRIPS. The projector has been set up before the class enters. A reliable pupil is ready to operate it. On the blackboard the teacher has written a number of key words, typical expressions, and questions for guidance.

The teacher gives a very brief introductory talk, in English or in the foreign language. The room is darkened and the presentation begins.

This may proceed in several ways. It can be a straight lecture, in the foreign language, by the teacher. Or, after each picture, a brief pause may be made for questions and comments by the students.

The teacher should speak distinctly and not too fast, stressing all key words and new expressions. The linguistic phase should always be paramount.

At the close of the lecture the shades are pulled up and the normal classroom situation is restored. If time permits, the pictures shown are discussed, preferably in the foreign language.

The assignment may be the writing of a composition on the subject of the filmstrip.

Subjects Taught with Pictures. Any theme or unit that involves concrete objects, animals, or human beings can readily be enlivened and vivified by the use of pictures—whether still, in the form of slides, filmstrip, or motion picture. In the elementary grades and in beginning classes still pictures will probably be found most useful. In upper grades and advanced classes the filmstrip and the motion picture will be more effective, especially for cultural topics. In beginners' classes the following topics can be taught with pictures:

1. Animals; five domestic, five wild. Names, colors, qualities (wild, strong, lazy, etc.); use (cow—milk), etc.
2. Flowers: five or six well-known. Colors.
3. Fruits: five or six. Colors; taste (sweet, good); origin.
4. Parts of body. (Teacher can point to himself or to students.)
5. Weather and seasons. Pictures of rain, snow, sun; of spring, summer, fall, winter; blowing wind.
6. Nature: mountain, valley; river, forest, plain.
7. Members of family: father, mother, son, daughter, grandfather, grandmother (age, activities, health).

8. Family at meal: dishes, foods, table conversation ("Please pass
   . . ." "Please give me more . . .")
9. Family at home in evening: various activities.
10. Rooms of the house: picture of each room; articles of furniture.
11. Articles of furniture: more detail.
12. Articles of clothing: male, female.
13. Vocations. (Word families; e.g., El panadero hace pan en la pana-
    dería.)
14. Dog and cat: pets; color, size, habits.
15. The garden: trees, flowers.
16. The farm: animals, occupations, products.
17. Means of transportation: railroad, steamboat, automobile, bus,
    streetcar, airplane, bicycle.
18. Sports: baseball, football, swimming, running, etc.
19. Travel: buying ticket, on train, on boat, on plane; with valises, at
    hotel.

Comic Strips

Among pictorial representations outside the classroom the comic
strip and the comic book are unquestionably among the most popular. They are enjoyed by old and young; there is hardly a magazine
or newspaper that does not offer them. In fact, they are so much in
demand that the comic book has become big business. It is said that
over twenty million copies are sold each month.

Educators have questioned the educational value of the newspaper comic strip and the comic magazine. Still, such media have encouraged tens of thousands of the unacademically minded to read
and to take an interest in literature. This is true not only in the
United States but also in other countries. In Mexico the comic book
was found to be the most effective way of teaching reading to illit-
erate masses. It is, after all, on a sound pyschological basis, consist-
ing as it does of a series of related pictures which tell a story.

ADVANTAGES OF THE COMIC BOOK. Those who would defend the use of
the comic book maintain that

1. Since it is easy to read, it encourages reading.
2. By introducing new words, it builds vocabulary.
3. The subject matter is entertaining and amusing; hence the
reader is attracted.

4. The plots of the narratives are similar to those of the films.

5. It is a very inexpensive medium.

USE OF COMICS IN FOREIGN LANGUAGES. Recognizing the fact that the urge to read comics is so strong, some educators are ready not only to tolerate them but to employ them for educational purposes. Some of these publications have risen to a higher artistic and literary level. There are now comic books portraying Bible stories and literary classics. In fact, the word "comic" has become a misnomer. Also, series of pictures are used in business, in advertising, in campaigns for the improvement of health and social conditions. During the war they were used to build morale.

Now there are even textbooks that contain comics. Their use in that instance is somewhat questionable, for the comic is something ephemeral whereas the textbook is rather permanent.

However, there are comic strips in the foreign language, in black and white, and in color. French ones can be obtained from Canadian newspapers; Spanish from Mexican and West Indian publications. These may be used, for the sake of entertainment and amusement, on the bulletin board. There is no harm in this. As Anatole France put it, "En s'amusant on apprend tout." The eager reader of the comic in the foreign language may pick up many a word and expression which would not interest him in the textbook.

The Motion Picture

A favorite device for teaching in the sciences, home economics, and vocational subjects is the motion picture. In these areas, for obvious reasons, it is eminently effective. Commercial concerns have realized this and have put out many interesting and informative films for school use. In foreign languages the film has been used largely as background or cultural material. With the present widespread use of audio-visual aids and with the renewed emphasis on the linguistic, the question arises: What use shall the foreign language teacher make of motion pictures? What are the advantages and disadvantages of this medium?

ADVANTAGES OF THE MOTION PICTURE. First and foremost, of course, is the fact that young and old like to see "movies." Television is but an extension and special adaptation of the motion picture. Both are extremely effective mass media; they can be used for entertainment and for education, for diversion and for instruction, for disseminating information and for influencing thinking. Educationally the advantages are these:

1. The motion picture holds attention. The sharp contrast of darkness and bright light; the isolation of the student from his fellows; the movement and rapid change in the picture compel almost complete attention. There is a double impact of sight and sound.

2. Motion, sound, and color heighten reality. Especially in presenting life in the foreign country, nothing is more effective and interesting than a good motion picture. It is informative, instructive, emotional, and stimulating.

3. The motion picture extends widely the horizon of the student. Not even the most fascinatingly written book can portray the foreign scene, the historic event, the biographical details with the vivacity and warmth of a good motion picture.

4. The motion picture provides a common experience for all pupils. Even the slowest and dullest can see and get something out of a picture, whereas deficiencies in reading would prevent optimum use of a book. The intelligent pupils will, of course, see more and more accurately.

5. Probably better than any other medium the motion picture can teach the imponderables. Attitudes, interests, ideals are built up more easily and almost unconsciously through the showing of the proper motion pictures. In foreign language teaching we want to inculcate broad-mindedness, tolerance, sympathy, and understanding.

DISADVANTAGES OF THE MOTION PICTURE. As in the case of other audiovisual devices, the motion picture also has several drawbacks:

1. A film must be chosen with reference to its effectiveness in a given situation. For presenting cultural background, showing the landscape, the industries, the occupations, etc. of the foreign country the motion picture is ideal. On the other hand, the film cannot be used for the bulk of linguistic training.

2. Films must be graded, especially if the foreign language is involved. For beginners only those should be used in which the speech is simple, clear, and slow. The extent of the vocabulary will have to be watched.

3. The motion picture has all the advantages and also the disadvantages of a group device. It is not recommended where individual teaching is paramount.

4. The motion picture is comparatively expensive.

5. There are often administrative and technical difficulties.

HOW TO USE THE MOTION PICTURE EFFECTIVELY. For certain purposes the motion picture is a very effective means of teaching. To secure optimum results

1. The teacher should be acquainted with the films that are available. This means looking through lists and catalogues and becoming familiar with possible sources. In bigger cities these will consist of museums, foreign government travel bureaus, universities, private organizations, commercial enterprises, and the service bureaus of language associations. Larger school systems, too, maintain collections of films and other audio-visual materials.

2. The best physical conditions should prevail for the showing. Attention should be paid to satisfactory seating, so that every student may be able to see and hear in comfort.

3. Someone who is skilled in operating the projector should be present—either the teacher or a technician. The machine should, of course, be set up properly. The film must be threaded and the sound adjusted; the shades should be drawn and the lights turned out.

4. The class should be prepared for the showing. This involves

(a) motivating the film

(b) discussing the background

(c) anticipating vocabulary difficulties

(d) indicating what is to be looked for

(e) preparing a number of questions to be answered.

5. There should be a follow-up of the showing. The questions will be answered and the contents discussed.

The Foreign Language Film. Until very recently only a limited number of films for instructional purposes have been available in foreign languages. Most of these have been in either French or Spanish; there is a lesser number in German and Italian. In Hebrew and Latin there are extremely few. Also, they are rather uneven in value, linguistically and informationally. They range all the way from the fairy tale in beginner's French to the travelogue. A glance at even a shorter annotated list will indicate how necessary it is to make a careful selection.

Heretofore the foreign language film was thought of largely as background material, that is, useful for presenting scenes in the foreign country. In beginners' classes the sound was in English; in more advanced classes it was in the foreign language. It then became a test of comprehension.

More thought, however, should be given to the use of the motion picture for teaching the foreign language. Since this idea is so new, very little material is available. There are a few films in which travel abroad is depicted. The objective is to project the student into the foreign country and to give him ample practice in the foreign language in the foreign environment.

The enterprising teacher can also take a silent film and by the use of the tape recorder let his own students provide the dialogue in the foreign language. This is an excellent project. When the film is shown in class, all students in the room are asked to repeat the dialogue in unison as the action proceeds. This provides wonderful practice, for the conversation is at normal speed and the student is compelled to maintain a given pace. Watching the action at the same time comes close to making the student an actual participant in the scene.

Training the Teacher How to Handle a Projector

The following suggestions are given by the Victor Animatograph Corporation of Davenport, Iowa.

The know-how of operating a 16-mm. sound motion-picture projector can be properly acquired only by doing. Consequently, instruction is of maximum effectiveness when limited to two trainees during each instruction period.

When larger groups must be taught, it is essential that either more instruction periods be scheduled or more projectors be made available.

If several projectors are employed for co-ordinated instruction of a group, the ratio of two trainees per projector should be observed. Up to eight trainees may thus be taught by one instructor with four projectors.

The projector should be placed upon a rigid stand 20 to 46 inches high, thus providing convenient access for threading and operating. Where several projectors are employed, each should be placed on a separate similar stand, the stands spaced approximately five feet apart and faced in a single direction.

A jumbo photographic enlargement, or blowup, of the projector, in which the route of film travel is clearly shown and the nomenclature of important parts indicated, should be posted adjacent to the projectors. This will serve as an effective training aid.

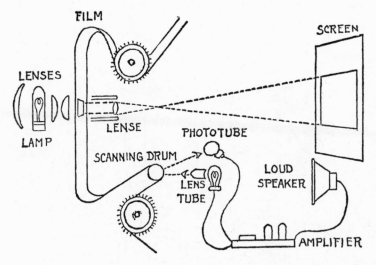

HOW THE 16 MM MOTION PICTURE PROJECTOR WORKS

It is generally found that in the case of class groups two or three hours are required for instruction, with another two hours spent in supervising practice. It is best to have the instruction period in the morning and the practice period in the afternoon.

At the conclusion of the course, the trainee should be given a test. If he fails to secure a passing grade, he is required to return for further instruction until the operation has been fully mastered.

If the trainee attains a passing grade, he is assigned to his superior for approval. Upon completion of three separate showings satisfactorily handled, his superior should certify to this effect and the certification thereafter qualifies the trainee as an approved projectionist.

Conversation Based on a Picture

(Spanish)

PREPARACIONES PARA LA EXCURSIÓN

The picture shows members of the family in the kitchen preparing lunch for the outing. (Based on Unit XV of *La Vida Diaria* by Huebener and Finocchiaro.)

The unit has been read; the new words have been learned; the exercises have been done. The next day conversation is carried on. As a basis the picture on page seventy-five is taken or, better, and enlargement displayed before the class.

The teacher asks questions about the picture; individual pupils answer. After each one has spoken, he writes his answer on the board below the answer of the pupil who preceded him. Since the questions are sequential, a composition will result. This is an excellent way of summarizing the lesson.

54

Teacher's Questions	Pupils' Answers
1. ¿Qué día de la semana es? ¿Van los niños a la escuela? (¿Cómo sabe Vd.?)	Hoy es sabado y los niños no van a la escuela. (Miro el calendario en la pared.) Es temprano. (Miro el reloj de pared.) Hay
2. ¿Es tarde? (¿Cómo sabe Vd.?)	gran actividad en la cocina. La
3. ¿Qué hay en la cocina?	familia se prepara para pasar el
4. ¿Qué hace la familia?	día al aire libre. Creo que van al
5. ¿Adónde van?	parque zoológico. La madre pre-
6. ¿Qué prepara la mamá?	para emparedados de jamón y de
7. ¿Qué hace la abuela?	queso. La abuela fríe los pollos
8. ¿Qué hace la hija?	en la estufa. La hija lava las fru-
9. ¿Qué hace el hijo Pedro?	tas y los vegetales frescos. El hijo
10. ¿Qué hace el padre?	observa a la abuela. El padre
11. ¿Están todas las personas ocupadas?	toma el cesto del armario. Toda la familia está ocupada. El único
12. ¿Quién es el único que no trabaja?	que no trabaja es el perro.

To add to the interest the teacher may inject an occasional aside. The answer to this need not be included in the composition.

If it is evident that the pupils are not quite familiar with the new vocabulary, the teacher should write on the board the words she supplies.

After the composition has been completed, it is inspected for errors and read aloud.

Teaching the Names of Animals
(Spanish)

The teacher has pictures of five domestic and five wild animals: dog, cat, horse, cow, donkey, lion, tiger, elephant, bear, and monkey.

He shows the picture of each of the domestic animals first and names them. Then he asks, "¿Qué es esto?" and calls on pupils for the answer. Then he makes the statement, "El caballo es un animal doméstico." The question will be, "¿Qué es el caballo?"

Then he may ask questions as to color, size, etc. New expressions might be "El burro es perezoso. El caballo trabaja. La vaca da leche. El gato bebe leche, etc."

A pupil may hold the pictures and ask the questions.

A personal reference may be brought in by asking, "¿Tiene Vd. un perro, un gato? ¿Cómo se llama?"

As a summary a little composition can be built up. Various pupils will contribute one sentence each. A board monitor will write them on the board under one another. E.g.:

Tengo un gato. Es blanco. Es pequeño. Bebe leche. Algunas veces come carne. Duerme en el sofá. Es un animal simpático. Me gusta.

The pictures of the wild animals can be treated in the same way.

El tigre es un animal salvaje. ¿Qué es el tigre?

Sample compositions:

El tigre es un animal feroz. Vive en el bosque. Come carne. Es grande. El pequeño gato es su primo. Me gusta el gato. No me gusta el tigre feroz.

El elefante es muy grande. Tiene grandes orejas. Tiene una trompa grande. El elefante salvaje vive en el bosque. El elefante doméstico vive en la aldea. Trabaja. Es muy útil.

El mono es un animal salvaje. Vive en el bosque. Come frutas y nueces. Hay monos en el jardín zoológico. Son cómicos. Me gustan.

Use of Charts

(Italian)

"LA FAMIGLIA"

(Lesson based on Chapter I of Masella and Huebener's *Learning Italian*, published by Henry Holt & Co., New York.)

The chart on p. 59, in enlarged format, is displayed in front of the class. The teacher asks questions according to the following patterns. (This may also be done by tape recorder.) Individual pupils answer the questions, as the teacher points to the chart.

I. Come si chiama?

1. Come si chiama questo signore? Questo signore si chiama Roberto.
2. Come si chiama questa signora? Questa signora si chiama Maria.
3. Come si chiama questo ragazzo? Questo ragazzo si chiama Riccardo. Etc.

II. Chi è?

1. Chi è? È Riccardo, il fratello di Carolina.
2. Chi è Carolina? Carolina è la sorella di Riccardo.
3. Chi è Roberto? Roberto è il padre di Riccardo. Etc.

WAS IST DAS?

DAS IST DER BÄR

DAS IST DAS KAMEL

DAS IST DER WOLF

DAS IST DER AFFE

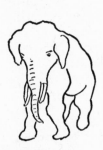

DAS IST DER ELEFANT

DAS IST DIE GIRAFFE

DAS IST DER TIGER

DAS IST DER LÖWE

QUÉ HACE EL MUCHACHO?

EL VA A PIE

EL CORRE

EL SALTA

EL CAE

EL ENTRA

EL SALE

EL SE PASEA EN BICICLETA

EN CABALLO

EN AUTOMOVIL

EN SCUTER

III. Alcuni posizioni.

1. Chi è alla sinistra di Roberto? Maria è alla sinistra di Roberto.
2. Chi è alla destra di Francesco? Rosa è alla destra di Francesco. Etc.

With a little ingenuity the teacher can introduce a large number of substitutions in these patterns. The pupils must, of course, be familiar with the characters represented, so that they can refer to them with ease. Briefly they are: Francesco and Rosa, grandparents; Roberto and Maria, parents; Riccardo and Carolina, the children.

As indicated, the question sequence can center around the names of the various members of the family, their relationship to one another, and their positions in the picture. Each one can also introduce himself by saying:

Io sono Riccardo. Sono il fratello di Carolina. Sono il figlio di Roberto e di Maria. Sono il nipote di Rosa e di Francesco. Sono Riccardo.

The other objects in the picture—the tree, the house, the gate, the flowers, the table, the dog, etc. may be used for conversational purposes. A final summary might consist of a series of sentences, in answer to questions, written on the board in logical sequence to form a composition describing the activities of the family in the garden.

Visual Materials and Techniques / 59

[III]

Audial Materials
& Techniques

HISTORICAL BACKGROUND

IN VIEW OF the rapid strides made in the field of applied science during the past century, it is amazing that the use of mechanical devices was so late in reaching the classroom. Within the past three decades the market has been flooded with foreign language records; previously there was comparatively little available in that field. And what was available was intended for the adult self-learner who listened to the records at home in the evening. There were no records intended for pupils learning a language in the classroom. The paucity of recorded material is all the more surprising when one considers that the phonograph was invented by Edison in 1877 and that the human voice was featured right from the start.

The widespread use of phonograph records for teaching foreign languages did not really come about until the Army Specialized Training Program was set up. This educational experiment, more than any other factor, was responsible for the interest in and enthusiasm for learning a language by listening to records.

LEARNING

THE AUDIAL APPEAL. Audio-visual techniques are based on the generally accepted fact that the senses reinforce each other as avenues of learning. Since language is essentially sound, the audial appeal should be used first in teaching. After a fairly correct pronunciation has been established, the student may be exposed to the written and printed symbols. The order "audio"—"visual," then, is quite logical as far as language learning is concerned.

CHILD LEARNING. Starting with hearing first has sometimes been justified on the basis of a child's learning of his native language. To a limited extent it is profitable to study the child's approach to the vernacular. Typical is his persistence; his constant repetition of a new word until he has mastered it. Actually, this is learning by trial and error—a wasteful and uneconomical procedure.

Furthermore, the young child cannot give his reaction to the new words and expressions; he can tell us nothing about his learning. Also, he has plenty of time. The child learning his native tongue is surrounded by it all the time during his waking hours—at home, in school, in the street. Even before he is conscious of the nature of language he is exposed to the endless chatter and prattle that a mother talks to her baby. This continuous baby talk enters the child's subconscious mind and forms the basis for his later understanding of the language. The importance of this mother-to-baby chatter is demonstrated by the comparative speech retardation shown by children brought up in orphanages and institutions, where the normal expression of a mother's affection is lacking.

Summarizing, then, one may say that a child's learning his native tongue is characterized by

1. Plenty of time.
2. The natural order—aural, oral, reading, writing.
3. Unlimited daily practice in practical situations.
4. Intense motivation.

LIMITATIONS OF THE CLASSROOM. The training of the child's ear through the constant flow of speech which surrounds him from infancy on cannot be imitated in the artificial atmosphere of the schoolroom. The great limitations are those of time and experience.

However, although the student of a second language lacks the constant flow of speech to which the child learner is exposed, he has certain advantages to compensate for these lacks.

STUDENT LEARNING. The one great advantage is that the student has already learned a language, his native tongue, which can be used as a basis for reference and comparison. In other words, he has already formed speech habits. This is only a partial advantage, for in learning a second language he is faced with the task of acquiring the speech habits of another people. The skillful teacher, however, will capitalize on the student's linguistic apperceptive mass. Fluency in the new language is an important aim and the learning situation may be so arranged that, as in his native tongue, the learner has many experiences in listening.

Characteristics of the Learner of a Second Language. Outstanding are the following factors which differentiate him from the child learner:

1. Age—anywhere from childhood to old age.
2. Linguistic skill—his motor mechanics have been developed.
3. Intelligence—he has an awareness of what he is doing.
4. Setting—he usually does not live in the foreign milieu.
5. Motivation—may be of various kinds.
6. Opportunities for practice—limited.
7. Interest—varies.
8. Continuity—not always assured.

USE OF THE FOREIGN LANGUAGE. A listening situation for a studied language faces the basic difficulty that each situation must be staged or simulated. There is innate compulsion to use the second language. Both teacher and student may tacitly agree to use only the foreign language and artificially suppress the vernacular, but it does not always seem natural.

This does not mean that a language cannot be taught by the direct method. Every good language teacher has demonstrated the effectiveness of the use of the foreign language. The skill of the teacher resides in his setting the stage with a verisimilitude that is so convincing that the student is induced to speak with a considerable degree of naturalness. A powerful incentive is the assurance that sooner or later the student will be able to speak the language with ease. The deferring of present to future utility depends upon the skill and persuasiveness of the teacher.

The Relationship of Visual to Audial. As has been stated above, some authorities believe that the major part of our learning is through the eye. And since language is based primarily on sounds, the appeal must be an audial rather than a visual one. In the past much was made of imitating mouth positions in connection with pronunciation and there are still motion-picture courses which begin with this type of exercise. An expert like Emma Marie Birkmaier, however, believes that children's ears are more sensitive than adults' and that the use of visual aids in this connection is not necessary.

By and large, the audial aids seem to be reserved for the linguistic aspect and the visual aids for the cultural. In most discussions of the language laboratory, for instance, the motion picture and the filmstrip are not mentioned. The strength of these two visual aids undoubtedly lies in their ability to give the student a simulated experience in the foreign country. On the other hand, the picture, the film, and the motion picture can be used effectively for the linguistic aspect. The visual aid strengthens the impression of the foreign word by showing what the object or action looks like. Furthermore, it will be more authentic. A French *fenêtre* looks quite different from an American "window"; a German *Dorf* is not an American "village." In the elementary school, in high school, and in college the visual representation will enrich concepts and facilitate language learning.

LISTENING

ACCORDING TO the fourfold aim of language teaching, the various phases of acquiring a foreign tongue are listening, speaking, reading, and writing. Now, listening seems, on the surface, to be a very simple, passive, receptive process. Actually it requires attention, concentration, and application if it is to be effective. Hearing a language spoken every day does not necessarily lead to correct pronunciation and accurate speech. We have around us countless numbers of foreigners who have lived the major part of their lives in the United

States and still speak a very inadequate English. The fact is that they have never listened with concentration and have never tried to analyze what they have heard.

Pupils must be trained to listen critically as well as conversationally; there must be an attitude of concentration as well as appreciation.

TEACHING HOW TO LISTEN. Listening is a skill which can be developed by the teacher. The child is continually subjected to sound. In our modern age of highly developed techniques in communication—radio, movies, television—children spend a good deal of their time in listening to mass media. To make this listening effective, education must develop the critical and discriminating sense in the child.

The following are some ways of doing so:

1. See to it that the atmosphere in the classroom is conducive to listening. The room should be quiet; the seats should be comfortable. The listeners should not be too far from the speaker.

2. An aim should be set up for the listening. This aim should be clear to the class.

3. Encourage the pupils to ask questions about anything they do not understand.

4. Prepare the class for any activity that requires listening. Recall familiar facts, tell what is to be heard and what is to be particularly noted.

5. The material should be suited to the age, interests, and intelligence of the class.

6. Point out how meaning may be affected by gesture, facial expression, inflection, and emotion.

7. Provide opportunities for reproducing or summarizing what has been heard.

8. Maintain an audience situation.

9. Train the pupils to listen critically. The spoken word carries more force than the printed word.

THE PHONOGRAPH RECORD

WHAT TO USE RECORDS FOR. Phonograph records may be used effectively for a number of different kinds of listening in the foreign language classroom. They may be employed in the teaching of

1. Appreciation of the music of the foreign country.

2. Appreciation of vocal selections in the foreign language.

3. The singing of a song.

4. New vocabulary.

5. A dialogue to be memorized.

6. The appreciation of literary selections in the foreign language.

7. Aural comprehension. A prose selection is played and then questions are asked to see whether the pupils understood what was said.

8. Dictation. The selection is played three times: to give (a) a general idea of the content, (b) the actual dictation, at slower speed, in thought groups, and (c) at normal speed for checking the written work.

9. Culture.

ADVANTAGES OF RECORDS. Phonograph records possess a number of distinct advantages over radio programs. A record can be

1. Stopped at any point for questions, comments, and disscussion.

2. Repeated any number of times.

3. Played at any time desired and thus be introduced when it is most effective.

4. Pre-heard and evaluated. This is particularly important for the teacher in preparing himself.

5. Made for a given purpose in or by the school. The machine can be used for transcribing radio broadcasts or for recording pupils' voices. (This has become much easier and less expensive through the use of tapes.)

6. Obtained on almost any subject, of any musical selection, in any language.

The phonograph record serves the ear as the picture serves the eye. It reproduces vicariously many experiences which otherwise could not be introduced into the classroom.

Types of Records. Discs come with recordings in speeds of 78, 45 and 33⅓ rpm (revolutions per minute). Diameters range from 7 to 16 inches. Most phonographs and playback machines can be adapted to the three speeds.

The most economical to use are the LP (long-playing) records, which rotate at a speed of 33⅓ rpm. Each side furnishes from 15 to 20 minutes of recorded material. Most modern records are HiFi.

The latest type of disc is the stereo record. If this is to be used, the teacher should be sure that the playback machine will take stereo.

CRITERIA IN SELECTING. In selecting phonograph records for the foreign language classroom each should be judged on the basis of the following criteria:

1. Clarity and distinctness of the spoken language.
2. Suitability for the classroom.
3. Level and difficulty of the vocabulary used.
4. The speed of the spoken language.
5. Correctness and authenticity of the foreign language.
6. Appropriateness for the purpose it is to serve.

TEACHING A SONG. The procedure to be followed in teaching a song by means of the phonograph is as follows:

1. The teacher introduces the song by commenting on its significance and value, where sung (if regional), and on the life of the author (if important).

2. The pupils look at the words of the song on the blackboard or on mimeographed sheets. The teacher reads the text aloud; the class follows with concert reading. The teacher points out cases of elision and linking. (These should be indicated with diacritical marks.)

3. The meaning of each line is elicited; the teacher supplies the meaning for new words. The entire stanza is read again, with expression.

4. The record is played on the phonograph. The class listens.

5. The disc is played again. The class sings together with the record. The teacher comments, criticizes, makes corrections. She points out where the volume should be increased or diminished. The class is encouraged to make an improved effort.

6. The record is played softly; the class sings.

7. The class sings the song without the record.

ILLUSTRATIVE LESSONS

Teaching a Song with a Phonograph Record
(French)

"LA MARSEILLAISE"

1. The teacher introduces the selection.

"Today we are going to learn *La Marseillaise*, the French national anthem. It was composed in 1792 by Rouget de Lisle in Strasbourg. The mayor of that town asked his friend, the young captain and musician, to compose a song to inspire the soldiers who were to fight in the Republican Army. Rouget worked all night on the words and music. At seven o'clock next morning he had completed his composition. He dashed with it to the house of a fellow-officer and sang the song to him. The officer was thrilled. Together they went to the mayor's house. While the mayor's pretty niece played the piano, Rouget sang the stirring hymn. His hearers became wild with enthusiasm and soon the song was on everyone's lips.

"Among the volunteers that arrived in Paris soon thereafter was a regiment of men from Marseille. As they marched on the royal palace of the Tuileries they sang the rousing song. Because of this the Parisians named it 'the Marseillaise.' It is not only the national anthem of France, it is the international hymn of freedom.

"The army of the Republic was led by General Dumouriez; it consisted largely of enthusiastic but untrained troops. The enemies were the Prussians and Austrians, seasoned soldiers, led by the Duke of Brunswick. They managed to cross the Rhine and capture Verdun. Paris seemed within easy reach. But suddenly the tide turned. The French were victorious in the battle of Valmy in September, 1792, and the enemy was driven back across the Rhine."

2. The pupils look at the text, which is either on the blackboard or on mimeographed sheets. Elision and linking are indicated. The teacher points out each instance. The teacher reads the words aloud, slowly and distinctly.

Allons‿en - fants de la Pa - tri - e,
Le jour de gloire‿est‿ar - ri - vé;
Con - tre nous de la ty - ran - ni - e,
L'é - ten - dard san - glant‿est le - vé,
L'é - ten - dard san - glant‿est le - vé.
En - ten - dez - vous dans les cam—pa - gnes,
Mu - gir ces fé - ro - ces sol - dats?
Ils vien - nent, jus - que dans nos bras,
E - gor - ger nos fils, nos com - pa - gnes.
Aux‿ar - mes, ci - toy - ens!
For - mez vos ba - tail - lons!
Mar - chons, mar - chons; qu'un sang‿im - pur a - breu - ve nos sil - lons!

3. The meaning of each line is elicited. A bright student can be called upon to translate the whole stanza. The teacher supplies the meaning of new words. These will probably include the following:

étendard	campagnes
sanglant	citoyens

mugir   sang impur (san-kam-pür)

égorger   abreuve

                                        sillons

4. The record is played. The class listens.
5. The record is played, the class sings with it. Teacher comments.
6. The record is played softly; class sings.
7. The class sings the song without the record.

Teaching a Song with a Phonograph Record
(German)
"Die Lorelei"

1. The teacher introduces the selection.

"Today we are going to learn one of the best-known German songs, 'Die Lorelei.' It is by Heinrich Heine, the poet who was born in Düsseldorf on the Rhine but who lived, married, and died in Paris. His *Buch der Lieder* contains many beautiful poems, some of which have been set to music.

" 'Die Lorelei' is the name of a song and of the mythical siren seated on a promontory of the same name at St. Goarshausen on the Rhine. The legend of the blonde nymph enticing sailors probably stems from the fact that smaller vessels often foundered in the treacherous whirlpools at the base of the Lorelei rock."

2. The pupils look at the text, either on the blackboard or on mimeographed sheets. The teacher reads the words aloud, slowly and distinctly.

> Ich weiss nicht, was soll es be - deu - ten,
> Dass ich so trau - rig bin,
> Ein Mär - chen aus al - ten Zeï - ten,
> Das kommt mir nicht aus dem Sinn.
> Die Luft ist kühl und es dun - kelt,
> Und ru - hig fliesst der Rhein;
> Der Gip - fel des Ber - ges fun - kelt
> Im A - bend - son - nen - schein.

3. The meaning of each line is elicited. A bright student will be called upon to translate the stanza. The teacher takes up certain words for special study.

Sinn   Gipfel

dunkeln   funkeln

4. The record is played. The class listens.
5. The record is played again; the class sings with it.
6. The teacher goes over the words of the second stanza.

> Die schön - ste Jung - frau sitzet
> Dort o - ben wun - der - bar,
> Ihr gold - nes Ge - schmei - de blit - zet,
> Sie kämmt ihr gol - de - nes Haar.
> Sie kämmt es mit gol - de - nem Kam - me,
> Und singt ein Lied da - bei,
> Das hat ei - ne wun - der - sa - me
> Ge - wal - ti - ge Me - lo - dei.

7. The meaning of each line is elicited. The entire stanza is trans-lated by a student. Certain words are given special attention.

Jungfrau	wundersam—wunderbar
Geschmeide	gewaltig
blitzen	Melodei for Melodie (forced rhyme)

8. The second stanza is played. The class listens.
9. The class sings the second stanza.
10. The class sings the entire song.

Teaching a Song with a Phonograph Record
(Spanish)

"Adiós, Muchachos"

1. The teacher introduces the selection.

"Today we are going to learn the song of a cowboy, but not an American cowboy. Not only in our country but also in Europe—and that has come chiefly through the motion picture—the cowboy is associated with Indians and the wild West. That has produced an entire literature and a rich repertory of songs.

"But there is a type of cowboy in South America who also has inspired the author and the artist. That is the colorful gaucho. There are many stories and pictures and songs about him.

"The selection we are going to study this morning is the farewell song of an Argentine cowboy who is obliged to retire from his active life. Sadly he takes leave of his comrades; with nostalgia he recalls the good old times.

"Since cattle raising is one of the leading industries of Argentina, the gaucho has been a typical figure of the vast pampas, the grassy plains. Like our cowboy, he plays a romantic role in song and story.

Roaming the endless pampas, the gauchos used to gather at ranch fiestas to sing and to dance. The wandering minstrel cowboy, called the *payador,* composed ballads to his guitar and engaged in song contests with rival singers.

"According to one legend, the fearless Santos Vega challenged a mysterious dark-skinned stranger to a contest. For three days and nights they played and sang. Finally, the listening cowboys decided that the stranger was the better of the two. Sadly Santos Vega rode away over the plains, never to return."

2. The pupils look at the text on the blackboard or on mimeographed sheets. The teacher points out where linking occurs. She reads the stanza aloud.

A - diós mu - cha - chos com - pa - ñe - ros de mi vi - da,
Ba - rra que - ri - da de‿a - que - llos tiem - pos
Me to - ca‿a mí hoy em - pren - der la re - ti - ra - da,
De - bo‿a - le - jar - me de mi bue - na mu - cha - cha - da.
Adiós, mu - cha - chos, ya me voy y me re - sig - no
Con - tra‿el des - ti - no na - die la ta - lla,
Se ter - mi - na - ron pa - ra mí to - das las fa - rras,
Mi cuer - po‿en - fer - mo no re - sis - te más.
A - cu - den a mi men - te re - cuer - dos de‿o - tros tiem -
    pos,
De los be - llos mo - men - tos que‿an - ta - ño dis - fru - té
Cer - qui - ta de mi ma - dre, san - ta vie - ji - ta
Y de mi no - vie - ci - ta que tan - to‿i - do - la - tré.
Se‿a - cuer - dan que‿e - ra her - mo - sa,
Más be - lla que‿u - na dio - sa y que e - brio de‿a -
    mor
Le dí mi co - ra - zon, mas el Se - ñor, ce - lo - so de sus
    en - can - tos
Hun - dien - do me‿en el llan - to me la lle - vó.
A - dió mu - cha - chos, etc.

3. The meaning of each line is elicited. A bright student is called upon to translate the entire stanza. The teacher supplies the meanings of new words. The following may have to be explained:

barra	tallar	cerquita
me toca a mí	farras	noviecita
retirada	antaño	idolatré
alejarse	disfrutar	diosa
muchachada	celoso	ebrio
resigno	llanto	hundir

4. The record is played again. The class listens. It would be well too, to display the picture of a gaucho on his horse.

5. The record is played; the class sings with it. The teacher comments.

6. The record is played softly; the class sings.

7. The class sings the song without the record.

(See Appendix for list of recommended recordings.)

RADIO

The Educational Use of Radio. In view of the fact that almost every American home has a radio set, the broadcast is one of the most widely used mass media for communication. Its value in advertising was recognized almost from the start, and that phase of radio broadcasting will undoubtedly remain a permanent one in this country. The system of commercial sponsoring seems firmly established. In other countries, where the government maintains the stations, such sponsorship is not necessary; hence no "commercials."

Another very important aspect of radio, however, has declined, at least on the larger nationwide hookups. That is the purely educational broadcasts. Years ago both NBC and CBS offered nationwide programs, especially in music. These programs were specifically designed for the schools. But they were soon given up, partly because of the alleged indifference of school authorities and partly because it was difficult to fit the programs into the curriculum and the time schedule of the schools. Also, only a small proportion of the schools were equipped with receivers.

SCHOOL AND COLLEGE BROADCASTING. Curiously enough, there were many college radio stations, using an AM band, before commercial radio took over. At one time there were as many as a hundred; between 1930 and 1940 the number decreased. Some universities, however, developed their stations into a "School of the Air" which broadcast programs intended for the schools. The rest of the day was devoted to musical programs and adult education. Several midwestern states have distinguished themselves in this area, notably Ohio, Minnesota, and Wisconsin. The station of Ohio State University in Columbus is so powerful that it has a state-wide radius.

EDUCATIONAL PROGRAMS FROM LOCAL STATIONS. The great impetus to educational broadcasting came when the FCC instituted the FM educational band. This made it possible to secure a local station at moderate cost for educational broadcasting. There are such stations all over the country at present. They initiate only one fourth of their program, in general, the rest coming from tapes. These are circulated by NEAB throughout the country, which makes it possible for even the smallest and most obscure station to produce a first-class program. In fact, eight series are used throughout on NEAB. Tape is comparatively cheap; the multiple duplicator is now rather common. The growth of FM educational broadcasting has relieved the large nationwide stations of responsibility in this area.

PUBLIC SCHOOL RADIO STATIONS. A number of larger school systems maintain their own educational radio stations. Among the outstanding ones may be named: New York, Chicago, Cleveland, Detroit, St. Louis, Atlanta, Newark, San Francisco, and Portland (Ore.).

Smaller school systems can rely on "the school of the air" time— that is, the half hour allotted by FCC to educational programs.

The use of radio for educational purposes is, then, growing. Some local school systems can get along on a 10-watt transmitter. Some university stations, on the other hand, can reach the whole state.

EDUCATIONAL RADIO ABROAD. One of the oldest and most successful educational radio systems is that of the British Broadcasting Company. For many years programs have been produced for the teaching of foreign languages. Hearers are supplied with well-printed and illustrated booklets—manuals for the teachers and guides for the students. Germany, too, has maintained a number of fine educational radio programs. And the Soviet Union is using radio, as it does all other media of mass communication, for education and indoctrination.

In comparison, the situation in the United States has not been of the best. As reported by the chairman of FCC in 1952, only one fourth of the nation's schools were equipped with receiving sets and only about twenty states engaged in state-wide educational broadcasting. He pointed out that in England 98 per cent of the schools were equipped with radio.

ADVANTAGES OF RADIO. Radio possesses several distinct assets as a teaching device.

1. Since the broadcast depends on the human voice, emotion and feeling can be conveyed in a way that no printed text can do.

2. If the speaker is a distinguished person, or is in the news, there is an added thrill in listening to his remarks.

3. The realism of the broadcast can be increased by sound effects.

4. Authorities in any given field can speak on the program. In the case of languages, the native voice can be heard.

5. Radio programs are comparatively inexpensive.

6. Listening to specified commercial programs at home may be made a homework assignment.

DISADVANTAGES OF RADIO. As in the case of other audio-visual devices, radio, too, has certain drawbacks in the classroom.

1. Attention must be concentrated on listening. This requires a special effort on the part of pupils.

2. Radio is one-way communication. There is no room for comments or questions from the floor.

3. The radio program cannot be heard in advance and thus cannot be prepared for.

For teaching purposes, however, the advantages of radio seem to outweigh the disadvantages. The mere fact that the appeal is made solely to the ear eliminates the distractions which may ensue from the added visual appeal of the motion picture or of television. In some situations—and that is particularly true of language learning—the visual appeal is entirely unwanted. We want the learner to concentrate on hearing the foreign language.

Furthermore, the element of the dramatic is very strong in the radio dialogue. It is significant that of the forty-six educational television stations not one does a dramatic series. Here radio has the great advantage: it can produce the most elaborate drama without expensive props; it need rely only on the human voice and on sound effects.

FOREIGN LANGUAGES AND RADIO. The radio can be used effectively in the teaching of foreign languages. The programs must, of course, be graded. They must be based on the vocabulary and the idioms which the pupil is learning. The radio program lends itself satisfactorily to imaginary visits to the foreign country. In addition to dialogue, authentic music and dance rhythms can be introduced.

In larger metropolitan areas where there are daily radio broadcasts in various foreign languages, it is possible to use some of these in the classroom or assign them for listening at home. But there are a number of drawbacks in connection with commercial programs.

Some of the languages represented are not generally taught in school (Yiddish, Polish, Chinese); the speech is usually rapid and sometimes colloquial or dialectal (Puerto Rican Spanish); the "commercial" continually obtrudes.

Far more satisfactory are the educational programs sponsored by commercial concerns or specifically set up by boards of education. One of the most extensive of the latter is Station WNYE of the Board of Education of the City of New York, which provides daily broadcasts in all school subjects, under the directorship of James F. Macandrew.

Among these have been a number of programs in foreign languages, prepared by Remunda Cadoux. One of the most successful has been "Letter from Paris," a series of fourteen broadcasts in French.

The aim has been to cover the two main phases of language teaching: (1) the cultural, on the basis of a vicarious life experience in the foreign country, in this case Paris; and (2) hearing and speaking the foreign language.

Each student is provided with a copy of the manual before the broadcast. He reads the Summary, which introduces him to the contents of the program, and also the Questions, the answers to which he will get by listening to the broadcast. Later the teacher will review the answers with the class.

The Conversation consists of phrases that Joan teaches Bill during the program. The Conversation is reproduced almost exactly as written in the manual, in a natural manner, generally toward the end of the little drama. The Conversation occurs in French at a point in the program when Bill meets a French man or woman with whom he wishes to converse. The students are instructed to follow the words in the manual as they are spoken by the characters.

The Songs are added to enrich the flavor of the program. They are included chiefly for enjoyment. The students need not understand all the words.

At the end of the series the class will have gained an enjoyable insight into life in Paris, will have acquired a good stock of useful expressions in French, and will have learned a number of delightful songs.

Radio

(French)

"Le Jour Commence"

Summary

Bill and Joan Browning are living with a French family while Bill, an ex-GI, is studying music at the Conservatoire de Paris. Joan helps Bill get accustomed to French life. She explains about breakfast, working hours, etc. As Bill is to leave for an overnight trip to hear a special concert, she helps him learn some of the words he will need to know.

Questions Answered on the Broadcast

1. How does a French breakfast differ from an American breakfast?
2. How is French coffee different from American coffee?
3. What are the working hours of the average Frenchman?
4. How would you order your breakfast at a French hotel?

Conversation

French	English
1. Monsieur désire?	1. What would you like, sir?
2. Je désire un petit déjeuner complet, s'il vous plaît.	2. I should like a complete breakfast, please.
3. Du café au lait, monsieur? Un café crème?	3. Coffee with milk, or "café crème"?
4. Du pain grillé ou un croissant?	4. Toast or a sweet roll?
5. Un petit déjeuner américain.	5. An American breakfast.
6. Du jus d'orange.	6. Orange juice.
7. Des œufs et du jambon.	7. Ham and eggs.
8. Apportez un journal, s'il vous plaît.	8. Bring a newspaper, please.
9. Quel journal, monsieur?	9. Which newspaper?
10. *Le Monde,* s'il vous plaît. Merci.	10. *The World,* please. Thank you.
11. À votre service, monsieur.	11. At your service, sir.

Song

J'attendrai,
J'attendrai, le jour et la nuit,
J'attendrai toujours ton retour.

J'attendrai, car l'oiseau qui s'enfuit
Vient chercher l'oubli dans son nid.
Le temps passe et court,
En battant tristement
Dans mon cœur si lourd,
Et pourtant j'attendrai ton retour.

[IV]

The Tape Recorder

ADVANTAGES. A new resource is available to the language teacher to support oral memory as a book supports visual memory; this resource is the magnetic tape recorder. By placing on tape materials which he teaches, the teacher provides the student with a permanent reference for refreshing his memory as needed, when he wishes to recall the sound of the word.

Phonetic script, which is a visual translation of sound, is dead by comparison with the bringing to life of words, sounds, and sentences on tape. The taped word gives accurate pronunciation not only of sounds (not just descriptively, but by living example) but also of sentence rhythm and of intonation. In short, it repeats the native's way of using the language.

On the other hand, if the teacher, although not a native, has sufficient fluency to conduct the lesson in the foreign language, his speech acceptable in the classroom is no less acceptable when recorded on tape. Thus the tape satisfies several alternative needs or situations. Where the teacher is fluent and records his own speech, he provides a permanent reference to a model of the same quality

77

as he presents daily to the student. This is equally satisfactory when presented on tape. The sight of a microphone sometimes gives a feeling of professionalism and of permanence to taped materials and produces in some persons a sort of stage fright in recording. The impression prevails that what is recorded should be of professional quality, as that of the actor or lecturer.

Actually the teacher need have no such feeling. A parallel exists between the mimeographing of visually presented materials and the taping of audially presented materials. The easy erasure of tape and the possibility of immediate recording, should provide a more relaxed attitude toward the taping process.

FLUENCY ON THE PART OF THE TEACHER. There are many situations in which a competent teacher assigned to teach a foreign language lacks oral fluency. While this is not an ideal situation, we must be aware of the fact that it does exist in many parts of the country. It may be that the teacher learned the language thoroughly in a formal way but did not have sufficient opportunity to practice the spoken language. Or, the teacher may be in a small school where he is assigned to several subjects, including a foreign language. Again there is a lack of opportunity for oral use.

Speaking the foreign language with near-native fluency is highly desirable, but not all language teachers possess this skill. There are other phases of language learning which are of considerable importance and if the teacher can convey these successfully, we must be satisfied.

On the other hand, with the present stress on the spoken tongue, correct pronunciation is of paramount importance. This was not the case when the reading aim was generally accepted.

VALUE OF TAPE TO THE TEACHER. To the teacher who is not fluent in the foreign language, the tape recorder will be of inestimable value. The teacher may procure tapes which have been prepared commercially by experts or natives or by a fellow teacher who is a native. He can then present good model pronunciations of the new vocabulary, of idioms needing drill or review, of dictation, etc. During the playing, the teacher will devote himself to a critical evaluation of the imitation of the spoken language by the students. Being relieved by the tape, even the teacher whose own pronunciation is flawless can give his full attention to a checking of the students' efforts. The less fluent teacher, on the other hand, will unconsciously acquire fluency and correctness in pronunciation and intonation by imitating the tape himself.

VALUE OF THE TAPE RECORDER. The tape recorder is a valuable adjunct to the oral activities of the foreign language lesson.

The machine should be on the teacher's desk, open, connected, and ready to use during the entire period. Then, according to the type of lesson or the point to which the lesson has developed, the teacher will use the tape to play a previously recorded illustration or exercise, which the students can hear, imitate, and use as a model to repeat orally or which they will write down as a dictation exercise. The variants in types of tapes will suggest themselves as the teacher develops facility in their use.

Specifically, the tape is valuable in the following ways:

1. It extends the repetitive force of the teacher's voice beyond his own physical limitations. A tape can be used all day long if need be.

2. Voices other than that of the teacher can be brought into the classroom. This is extremely important. The student can thus hear male and female voices, young and old, native and American, regional and standard pronunciations.

3. The tape provides a permanent reference for sounds in the language. It is like the standard text or reference work in its relation to the visual aspect of the language.

The tape adds a new potential to listening. It makes listening available to the student at times other than when the teacher is present and is speaking. Of course, the effective utilization of this potential depends upon the arranging of supplementary practice time in school or at home. It may entail modifications in the course of study. In any case, the tape recorder is one of the most valuable devices that can be used in achieving the speaking aim.

THE TAPE RECORDER: THE MACHINE

THE TAPE RECORDER is essentially a machine for recording and reproducing sound electronically (see p. 92). This differentiates it from the phonograph disc, which is basically mechanical. To record sound, a groove is cut on a given surface.

In the case of the tape recorder, however, sound waves generate electric impulses which create magnetic patterns in the tape's iron-oxide coating. The recording is fixed immediately; there is no need to process it. When played back, the magnetic patterns are moved past the gap in the reproducing head. They generate tiny electric voltages which are amplified and fed to the loudspeaker. There is practically no wear. The tapes may be used almost indefinitely. On the other hand, the tape may be erased and re-used. This is done by passing the tape through the magnetic field of the erasing head, which obliterates the magnetic pattern. This in no wise injures the tape. Although tapes are quite durable and the recordings are permanent, some care must be exercised in handling them or damage may result. The tape may tear and the recording may be erased.

TECHNICAL ADVANTAGES OF TAPE. Some of the many advantages of tape recordings are these:
1. The recording is permanent.
2. It may be erased and the tape used again.
3. Tape recording has higher fidelity than ordinary shellac discs.
4. Tapes are economical.
5. They occupy less space than discs.
6. It is easy to identify sequences.
There is only one great drawback: to locate a particular spot, the tape must be wound forward or backward. But this has been overcome to some degree by fast forward and rewind controls.

MECHANICAL DETAILS. Although there are different makes and models of tape recorders, they all operate on the same basic principles. For example, they all operate on AC current only. If DC current only is available, a converter must be used.

The construction of the machine may differ as to details. For instance, the take-up reel may be on either the right or the left side. The tape may face in opposite directions.

The spools of tape may be wound with the coated side facing inward or with the coated side facing outward. This side is darker in finish; it must be in contact with the magnetic heads. The inward type is the more common.

There are two types of tracks: single and dual. In the case of the dual track, the tape is reversed by turning both reels over and changing to opposite spindles. Speeds differ, too. The higher the speed the greater the degree of fidelity. Some machines may be operated at several speeds. The usual speed is $7\frac{1}{2}$ inches per second.

USING THE RECORDER. Operating the machine is fairly simple, but there are a number of things to watch if trouble is to be avoided.

After the recorder has been set up, the power cord is attached (remember, AC only!). The socket may be at either end of the recorder. Next, the empty reel is placed on the take-up spindle. The small pin on the spindle must fit into any of the three slots.

Then the tape is placed firmly in the slot with the oxide coating facing the recording head. Next, the tape is fastened on the take-up reel. It is wound five turns to attach the tape securely; if it is left slack, there is danger that it may snap.

The reels must sit firmly on both spindles; the tape must run freely. If the tape has been placed with the wrong side out, it can be rewound to get it into the correct position.

Recording. The tape having been inserted properly, the machine is ready for recording. After the microphone has been attached, the power may be turned on. Sometimes the power switch is combined with the volume control. The volume, or tone, control knob should ordinarily be turned to maximum treble. The button is turned to the word "record" and the safety button is pressed.

Before making the recording, the speaker's voice may be tested by holding the button down. The volume should be adjusted if it is not correct. Different machines have various ways of indicating insufficient volume: a small neon light, a bulb, or a needle indicator. The absence of fluctuations indicates too low a volume; the closing of the gap indicates too high a volume. Proper volume is shown by fluctuating and an occasional closing.

A test recording can now be made by switching to "Forward" and pushing down the safety button. If the test is satisfactory, it may be terminated by switching to "Stop." The safety button will come up; this is the position for recording. When it is down, recorded material will be erased.

The test recording is played by switching to "Play," then to "Rewind," then to "Stop," and finally to "Forward." The tone may now be adjusted.

If the test is satisfactory, the recording may proceed. This is done by turning to "Rewind" and then "Stop." The volume is set correctly. Next the button is turned to "Forward" and then to "Record." When the safety button is depressed the machine is ready to record.

Listening is Not Enough. Listening is an activity that is applied in various ways. It is a satisfactory and pleasurable experience to listen to music. One does not expect to retain the accurate sequence of chords or even be able to reproduce the melody, with the sort of attention given by the casual listener. The expert may be able to do these things, but his sort of attention is different.

Listening to a play, one will not be able to reproduce the entire action accurately, yet occasional dramatic remarks may be remembered—a telling curtain line, for example.

Still another type of listening is known to all of us: the half-attentive listening one gives to a long-winded talker on the telephone. In this situation one is able to continue unrelated thinking while still giving sufficient attention to make appropriate remarks and responses to the uninteresting material being spoken at the other end of the wire.

The attention required of the language student is of quite another order. He must listen not only to the casual moment, but to remember, to recognize later, and to be able to reproduce.

It is therefore important to associate some type of activity with each situation requiring the student to listen. He may be required, as he listens, to

(1) repeat the identical material he hears
(2) read silently as he hears the material read
(3) provide answers orally to questions asked of him
(4) provide answers in writing to questions asked of him
(5) look at a picture which the tape describes, and identify objects on the picture as the tape mentions them. (This is suitable for development into a cultural lesson.)

TAPE TECHNIQUES CAN BE INCORPORATED IN THE LESSON. When the teacher has learned to handle the tape recorder easily, he is in possession of a valuable instrument for the improvement of instruction. He now faces the questions: What goes on the tape? What should the student hear when he listens? What does the teacher say that he repeats or answers? The answers to these questions determine the value as well as the type of utilization of the tape recorder.

With a little ingenuity the teacher can incorporate laboratory procedures in his present procedures. The teacher need not abandon all traditional practices. Since the tape recorder and the language laboratory make possible a more satisfactory achievement of oral and aural aims, they should be considered extensions of present procedures.

Tape and Textbook. The materials to be taped must be kept in definite relationship to the regular course of study. The most practical thing to do is to relate the recording on the tape to the content of the textbook, since this is the basis of the daily lesson. The taped materials should not be extraneous. They may be compared to mimeographed exercises prepared by the teacher to implement the textbook. The mimeographed sheet makes a visual appeal; the tape makes an audial appeal. It is, of course, necessary to determine what parts of the textbook lend themselves to audial presentation.

Conversational Materials. A foreign language course frequently begins with conversational practice. The teacher points to objects, names them, acts out situations and describes what he is doing, gives directions to follow, etc. The students listen, repeat, answer, and follow instructions. This activity is carried on without referring to the textbook.

This type of oral-aural approach is live, interesting, and stimulating. It cannot be continued too long, however. The pupil's memory cannot be relied on for accurate recall; there must be a record of some kind to take home. Also the pupil craves a view of the written symbols.

Here the tape performs the useful function of providing a permanent record and of helping the student to recall correctly. After working through the conversational material, the teacher records it on tape for daily review at the beginning of the period. He can add to the taped material as the amount of oral-aural work increases, certain that none of the orally presented material will drop out or be overlooked. The student may relax. He need not insist on a written record, since the oral record is available.

Students may even borrow tapes for home practice. Copies can be made for circulation. The original tape, however, should never go out of the possession of the teacher, since it is too easily erased or destroyed. The student need worry no longer about incorrect recall of the model pronunciation. By means of the tape he can listen any number of times to the sounds of the language just as he heard them originally.

ACTION ACCOMPANIES SPEECH. While the tape is being replayed in class, the teacher and the students can make the appropriate gestures, pantomime actions, point to objects, and thus strengthen the impression of the spoken word. The meanings of the words and expressions will probably be remembered more easily than the sounds themselves, so that the students will be able to carry out actions sooner than they can repeat the directions accurately. After a few weeks of this type of practice, the teacher may wish to begin work in the textbook.

Having completed the initial, purely aural-oral phase, the teacher begins the systematic presentation of the elements of the language. Although the teacher may use few or no grammatical terms, his work must be structured in his own mind so that the student will experience a progressive development in his grasp on the language, whether through a more flexible control over speech patterns or through a more complex control over grammatical forms.

TEXTBOOK EXERCISES. Does the type of exercise in the ordinary textbook lend itself to taping to provide additional practice?

Each textbook lesson usually includes a list of new words. The teacher may treat the vocabulary in a number of ways. Some of the words may be presented in vivid context, so that the pupil infers the meaning. To save time, on the other hand, the teacher may read the list aloud and have the class repeat in chorus. The words are then used in sentences. The teacher may devise the sentences and have the pupils repeat them. Or, he may get the students to respond to questions involving the new words.

Here again the tape may be used effectively. The pupils listen while the tape gives the new words, with a pause after each so that the class may repeat, while watching the list in the book. If the pupils are encouraged to listen to the vocabulary repeatedly they may even dispense with the visual reinforcement of the book. In reviewing, the time allowed on the tape for oral repetition can be used for writing the words, as in dictation. This type of practice supplements but does not replace the live presentation by the teacher. It also permits subsequent repetition by pupils requiring additional drill.

Reading and Tape. In almost all textbooks, a reading selection introduces each lesson. Sometimes the teacher gives a model reading of a few sentences, which are repeated by the class in chorus or by individual students. This may be followed by silent reading.

The tape can be utilized for both these types of reading. Even after the teacher's model reading, students may not be able to read fluently and accurately. If the reading passage is taped, the model is available for repeated contacts as needed, to remind the student of correct pronunciation, intonation, and inflection. Silent reading of material in which pronunciation difficulties have not been overcome is liable to result in poor reading habits. The student may dawdle, stumble over or ignore words he cannot pronounce. In sight reading the student encounters another obstacle: the difficulty of grouping words to make sense.

The tape recorder can supply a fluent, well-pronounced accompaniment to pace the student's silent reading. The spoken accompaniment to the silent reading effects several important results. It prevents dawdling, it gives the student the opportunity to hear the language correctly pronounced, and it assists in comprehension, which depends largely upon getting the meaning in phrase groups. Either part or all of a reading selection in the textbook may be taped: some parts to permit phrase by phrase repetition to improve skill in oral reading and some fluently to guide the silent reading. Both types may well be included in the same tape. Correct timing will be discussed later.

TEXTBOOK EXERCISES AND TAPE. Usually the reading selection in the textbook is followed by a questionnaire designed to get the student to use actively the subject matter he has just read. These questions are suitable for a taped exercise. The purpose of the taped exercise differs from the textbook exercise as treated traditionally. The latter seeks to test the student's ability to reproduce the content of the reading selection by means of correct answers to the questions. The answer may be given orally or in writing. The taped presentation is intended to develop fluent and accurate speech. The tape, therefore, provides the model not only of the question but also of the answer. Time is allowed for the student to answer the question. The tape immediately gives the correct answer, so that the student may verify his response and correct it.

Many textbooks include a variety of fill-in and completion exercises. This is suitable for visual presentation, but does not lend itself very well for audial presentation. Such exercises would prove confusing on a tape recording.

By the same token, translation exercises from English into the foreign language do not belong on tape. The student does not have to hear how the English sentence sounds; he sees it printed in the textbook.

MANIPULATION EXERCISES. On the other hand, certain exercises may be more effectively presented audially than visually. These are the so-called "manipulative" exercises. A model is given of the desired manipulation. The student reworks succeeding sentences on the basis of analogy to the model.

The direction may be: "Put the sentences in the plural." Or, "Give the sentences in the past tense." If grammatical terms are to be avoided, the direction may be: "Restate the sentences, beginning with 'Charles et Marie,' instead of, as in the model, with 'Charles'." Or, "Begin each sentence with 'hier' or 'demain,' making the necessary changes."

This type of exercise can become as basic to the taped exercise as the fill-in is in the case of the mimeographed sheet. Endless variations are possible, depending upon the topic of the lesson and the stage of advancement of the class.

Care must be exercised in using words and forms that involve silent endings in French. If changes are to be made, for example, in the form of the past participle, the change must be audible, e.g., écrit-écrite, vert-verte, bon-bonne, etc.

Aural Comprehension. The aural comprehension exercise is widely used as a testing device. As usually given, the student hears the selection read twice. Then he hears questions based on the selection which he is to answer in writing. This exercise lends itself very well to tape recording. There are several obvious advantages. The student who was absent can hear the tape. Also the student who had trouble hearing the tape can listen until it is clear to him.

PRACTICE IN LISTENING COMPREHENSION. The ultimate objective of training in aural comprehension is to develop listening comprehension to a degree usable outside the classroom. Exercises emanating from the text are but the first necessary step in developing this skill. In the beginning the student may find it difficult to understand what he hears. The more closely what he hears corresponds to what he sees the more easily he will understand. Progressive aural development is designed to lead the student to grasp the meaning of audially presented material with an immediacy comparable to his ability to grasp the sense of visually presented material.

The first stage in the logical sequence is the presentation of material audially, and then of the same material visually. The next step is aural presentation of material without the visual reinforcement. The memory of the visual presentation will assist aural comprehension.

A further step in disengaging aural from visual dependence is accomplished by presenting listening material not previously heard but on a similar level of difficulty—comparable to visually presented plateau readings. It should consist of fresh material, utilizing vocabulary and speech patterns previously encountered, but in new combinations. This constitutes the audial parallel for sight reading.

EAR AND SPEECH TRAINING. The steps in ear and speech training may be summarized as follows:

1. Immediate repetition of materials heard (these to be graded in regard to length of the phrase to be repeated after a single listening).

2. Response to materials heard, involving some change in word order or in sentence construction. The responses are to be graded in terms of the amount of change required. When a question is asked in the third person, the response requires a rearrangement of the subject and verb; the rest of the sentence is repeated as given in the question. Examples:

> "Pleuvait-il hier soir?"
> "Oui, il pleuvait hier soir."
>
> "Bereitet die Mutter das Abendbrot für die Kinder?"
> "Ja, die Mutter bereitet das Abendbrot für die Kinder."

When a question is asked in the second person, a greater amount of change is required in the answer. Thus

> "¿Hacía mal tiempo cuando Vd. volvió anoche?"
> "Sí, hacía mal tiempo cuando volví anoche."
>
> "Pleuvait-il quand vous êtes rentré hier soir?"
> "Oui, il pleuvait quand je suis rentré hier soir."

In the latter not only the word order but the words change in the answer.

3. Response to questions asking for information, where the question gives no clue to the answer. The respondent must supply the information in an originally worded response. Example:

"¿Dónde está Madrid?"
"Madrid está en el centro de España."

"Chi è il presidente d'Italia?"
"Il signor Saragat è il presidente d'Italia."

After the student has developed facility in this type of question and answer he is ready for the next stage.

4. Independent speech, in response to some stimulus other than a question, as, for instance, (a) taking the initiative in asking a question, (b) describing a picture, a photograph, or a visually presented situation, (c) uttering an original idea of abstract nature. Here the flexibility of speech must match the complexity of the student's thought. At the point where the learner can express his ideas to his own satisfaction he has achieved a good control of the foreign tongue.

Speed is important in listening with understanding. Complete comprehension means grasping meaning at high speed. Foreign films and radio broadcasts do not slow down to accommodate the beginner. Listening comprehension must, therefore, be distinguished from speaking comprehension. A vast amount of spoken material, carefully graded in speed, is indicated. Different types of practice are required for the development of the listening skill and the speaking skill.

Techniques of Tape Preparation. Ready-made tapes are available but the teacher will want to prepare tapes specifically designed to meet the needs of given teaching situations. As stated above, the preparation of tapes to supplement the audial phase of the lesson may be compared to the preparation of mimeographed material to supplement the visual phase, i.e., the textbook. The following basic considerations should be observed in preparing materials for taping.

1. CONTENT. (a) The tape should be self-contained as to directions. If the tape is to be used in conjunction with a given lesson in a specific book, the page, the exercise, and the title of the book should be stated at the beginning of the tape. If the tape gives practice in sentence structure, the type of practice should be announced, in as few words as possible. The student should be told what he is to do. One example should suffice.

(b) Grammatical or linguistic explanations in English should be definitely excluded from the tape. The foreign language should be used almost exclusively.

(c) Basic tapes should relate closely to the content of the course. The teacher may prepare a tape listing the new vocabulary of a lesson, asking questions based on the reading passage, asking questions of a general nature, etc. Or, a reading selection from the textbook or some of the exercises may be taped (observing the cautions stated above with regard to book exercises).

(d) Special tapes may be prepared to give practice or remedial drill as needed. In teaching a poem, the tape recorder offers the best way of setting a model in pronunciation, intonation, and expression.

2. TIMING THE SPOKEN MATERIAL. (a) There is a tendency in the classroom to speak too slowly, to overarticulate difficult sounds, in order to help the student to understand. Since the taped speech is available for numerous repetitions, such overemphasis is unnecessary. The teacher should speak at normal conversational speed. Repeated listening will result in complete comprehension.

(b) Phrase groups should be approximately four to eight words, depending upon the sense. Each phrase group, pronounced at normal speed, should be followed by a pause about twice the length of the phrase to be imitated. This permits the student to repeat and gives him a moment to think. It is important that the pauses for repetition take place between phrase groups and not between single words. As the competence of the student increases, the space can be reduced to the time required by the teacher to repeat the phrase. The teacher can check by articulating softly each phrase as he prepares the tape.

(c) For questions on tape double the time should be allowed which the teacher requires. Time allowance can be checked by having a student present while the tape is made.

(d) The primary aim of the tape is to develop fluency and accuracy. Hence, after the question has been asked and the time elapsed for the response, the tape may give the correct answer. This will enable the student to verify his reply.

(e) In dictation, two readings at different speeds should be given. The first is fluent; the second is given in phrase groups for writing. Since writing is much slower than oral repetition, the recording should be made so that even the moderately slow writer can follow.

3. LENGTH OF THE LESSON. The span of attention of the average pupil must be considered in planning the length of the tape. Fifteen minutes seems to be the optimum. This will permit rewinding, replaying, and discussion. Practice in repeating a vocabulary or idioms should be much shorter. The practice feature is the most important in the use of the tape recorder. This is vitiated if the lesson is so long that it is impractical to replay the tape.

4. GRADING THE TAPES. The ultimate goal of the aural-oral practice is, of course, to develop in the student the ability to understand the spoken language outside the classroom, in life situations, and to give him facility in expressing himself freely. From direct imitation the learner proceeds by various stages to spontaneous speech.

(a) At first materials are taken directly from the textbook. Direct imitation is required. The aim is to give familiarity through the ear to materials made familiar through the eye.

(b) Next, materials from the text are adapted. Variations are introduced. The responses should involve some manipulation. The teacher must be aware of the grammar involved. Patterns of word substitution are included.

(c) At this point materials unrelated to the textbook are introduced. They will be of the same level of difficulty.

(d) Finally, the student is introduced to material outside the textbook and the classroom. Interviews with native speakers, transcriptions of foreign radio broadcasts, etc. are presented. The objective is to expose the student to an entirely free listening and speaking experience.

Using Tapes for Testing. In view of the fact that the present emphasis in language learning is on listening and speaking, these skills must be tested, rather than reading and writing as in the past. Of the two basic skills, listening is easier to evaluate than speaking.

Listening tests may be of several kinds:

(a) Multiple choice exercises on a sheet on which the student selects the appropriate word, sentence, or phrase spoken on the tape.

(b) Multiple choice of English meanings of tape recordings.

(c) Dictation exercise. This is a more objective test of comprehension than that given by a live teacher. Overarticulation, gesture, facial expression, and lip reading are ruled out.

(d) Tape tells story. Students write out answers to questions based on it.

(e) Tape tells story. Students write out gist in English.

(f) Tape presents series of questions. Students check off correct answers on sheet.

(g) Various sounds in the foreign language are played. Students discriminate on sheet among similar sounds given phonetically.

(h) Different materials played at varying speeds to test degree of rapidity of comprehension.

Speaking tests are difficult to administer, especially with larger groups. However, the test may be so organized that all students may be tested within a class period. Each student goes to the microphone and records a one-minute sample of his speech. The teacher can rate it immediately. If the evaluating is done later, it will require an equivalent amount of running time. Each student's speech should be tested at least twice a term. Speech tests may require the student to read aloud, at sight, or to answer questions orally on the text. In the latter case, the answer tape should be separate from the question tape, so that the teacher need not listen to the questions asked of each student being tested.

The electronically reproduced materials do not, of course, replace the teacher. He will plan his lessons as before; he will determine to what extent the tapes are to be used.

The great advantage of the use of tapes lies in the identical experience in rehearing. This is possible only with a machine. Almost every teacher tends to introduce variations in tone and tempo to make it easier for the student to hear and understand. This vitiates the attainment of the desired goal, which is the immediate comprehension of the foreign language spoken at normal speed. The student who is at first bewildered by the rapid speech coming from the tape will understand it after he has heard it a number of times. Just as the textbook provides visual reinforcement, the tape provides audial reinforcement.

RECORDING THE PUPIL'S SPEECH. The audial approach should be implemented by the recording of the pupil's voice at given intervals during the term. The third or fourth week of the term in the beginning grade, and during the very first week in higher grades, every pupil's oral performance in the foreign language should be recorded. One minute should be allowed per student; an equivalent amount of tape should be run before the next pupil records. It may require one or possibly two tapes for the entire class. These tapes are put aside. Toward the end of the term each student records in the blank space, in the same order as the first recording. A playback usually furnishes dramatic evidence of growth in speaking ability.

ADDITIONAL PRACTICE. This recording at the beginning and at the end of the term is, of course, not adequate for practice in speaking. The students should record their speech several times during the term. Each student may speak into the microphone in turn, while the class listens. Or, alternatively, the teacher may set up the tape recorder in the department office, or in some other convenient place, in charge of the school's student audio-visual squad.

(See page 150 for bibliography and page 151 for list of vendors.)

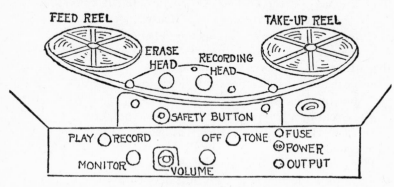

HOW THE TAPE RECORDER WORKS

[V]

Audio-Visual Techniques & the Classical Languages

IN VIEW OF the fact that the language laboratory stresses hearing and speaking, and in view of the fact that Latin and Greek are not usually spoken in the classroom, the teachers of the classics view the sudden enthusiasm over audio-visual devices with some misgivings. They are ready to accept the visual devices, and these for the enrichment of the cultural phase of classical studies, but are not attracted by the purely audial techniques.

The point of view of the teacher of the classics is expressed by J. Hilton Turner of Westminster College on pages 43–44 of "The Classical World" for November, 1959. He writes:

> It is part of the greater problem of the classicist that, where the modern language teacher may be able to justify his presence in a language laboratory with the use of simple repetition drills, possibly merely the recording of his text, the classicist will feel the need of drills which teach linguistic structure. The shortage of suitable com-

mercial material is crucial for both, but the modern language teacher has an abundance of records, usually of dubious adaptability, the classicist has very little of any kind. There are a few instructional records which contain readings from Latin or Greek literature, or conversational Latin.

The dim view of audio-visual techniques taken by the classics teachers does not seem to be justified. Perhaps the newer techniques are the very thing to bring new life to the teaching of Latin and Greek. In the early Middle Ages Latin was taught like a living language; the vocabulary, the idioms, and the expressions were those of everyday life. Latin was spoken, it was not just read. The Renaissance, with its stress on literary style, had a baneful effect on the teaching of Latin. The everyday language was replaced by Ciceronianism. The student had to struggle for years with the intricacies of grammar and syntax. The activity in the classroom was confined to reading and writing. This unhappy condition has prevailed up to modern times. It cast its blight on the modern languages, which in the beginning were taught in the same way. The wonderful work of Comenius—who originated the illustrated textbook with his *Orbis Pictus*—was ignored.

The restoration of spoken Latin in the classroom would be revolutionary. It would also give life and blood to a language which is so often referred to as "dead." The tape recorder and the language laboratory provide opportunity for practicing all phases of language study. If the classicist feels that he needs drills which teach linguistic structure, such exercises can easily be provided in Latin.

We need not attempt to convince the classics teacher of the usefulness of visual aids, for he is undoubtedly eager to use them to teach culture. But they, too, can be used for linguistic exercises, just as in the modern languages.

If the classicists indicate a greater desire for audio-visual aids in their field, it is quite certain that publishers will provide them.

THE LINGUISTIC TEACHING OF LATIN

WITH THE ADVENT OF audio-visual devices, a number of leaders in the field of Latin have realized the possible advantages of teaching that language by means of the tape recorder and the microphone. Materials for this purpose have been developed by Waldo Sweet in his Latin Workshop at the University of Michigan.

94

Although reading is still retained as the ultimate aim in teaching Latin, the principle is accepted that a language is essentially speech. Even though reading and writing are so important in Latin, it is felt that the fundamentals of the language can be taught more effectively by the use of orthophonic devices.

Grace Crawford, writing in the Yale *MAT Newsletter,* says:

> Forms and syntax are presented in contrast to English usage in complete, brief sentences in a pattern reading, and are drilled for mastery in pattern practice. The pattern practices are printed and studied partly from the page and partly from records to which the student may listen with earphones. In class the pupils recite answers to a tape recording of the same practice sentences. An answer on the tape, repeated after the student's answers, tells him whether he is right or wrong. The use of earphones is valuable for providing oral drill without disturbing others, for focussing concentration on the material at hand, and for speeding student responses in an impulse to "beat the tape" with perfect answers. . . .
>
> The reading material aims to be of sufficient interest to lead the student by a natural curiosity to "see how it comes out." . . . A great aid is the reading of a story first from a filmstrip in which the lines are given in sense units. By seeing only one line at a time the student is forcibly restrained from jumping around with the faulty jigsaw puzzle method. He is forced to read in Latin word order, observing the endings as keys to the organization of the sentence.
>
> . . . There is a naturalness and ease in the use of Latin orally. Students are reading more idiomatic Latin sooner and with considerable ease.
>
> . . . let us concentrate on the use of audio tools, tape recorder and records. The first requisite, of course, to the use of such tools is to integrate it completely with the routine learning—it is not a mere embellishment or distraction.
>
> Since any language is basically a spoken medium, even though our chief aim in Latin is to teach to read, we are making use of oral techniques for mastery of essential forms and usage, supplemented by some of the more usual types of written work. One of the chief devices is the pattern practice—a set of 20 or more sentences illustrating the point being taught. These are given in English, then Latin (or go from Latin to Latin) in the book, on records, and on tape. The student prepares them by listening to the record, at first with the book before him, then without it, doing his listening through earphones which both concentrate his attention and enable him to work in a room without disturbing others. The exercise is recited in class to the

tape recording, it being necessary for the student to say the answer in the interval provided before the tape gives the correct one. In this way it is possible for each pupil in a class of 25 to recite four times in ten to fifteen minutes. . . . More, rather than less "grammar" is actually learned, learned correctly—for the student does not practice his own errors but material which is correct—and learned in a meaningful context.

Here, then, is a medium which offers a real challenge to the creativity of the Latin teacher—to select and organize material, using groupings big enough to merit this type of treatment, either in anticipation of or review of material as presented in the text—to prepare exercises with minimum changes of vocabulary so as to concentrate on structure and with absolute grammatical and idiomatic accuracy.

[VI]

Television

IN BREAKING the lockstep of traditional procedures and methods, the teacher of foreign languages will find one of the most interesting new developments to be the use of television for the teaching of foreign languages.

Over a hundred foreign language teaching programs are being televised in the United States at present, showing the extent of interest in this new teaching medium.

There has been considerable discussion as to the value of such programs and the place they should occupy in a school's language program. Obviously, the value of the content must be decided in terms of the specific program under consideration.

ADVANTAGES OF TV. In considering the introduction of the televised program as a medium of instruction, the school should be aware of the following advantages:

1. Interest and appeal resulting from the novelty of the medium. Students connect television with pleasurable expectation and a positive feeling-tone.

2. Television provides a variant from the regular teacher's voice and techniques.

3. The televised lesson is not subject to the digressions, irrelevancies, or interruptions which sometimes occur in the usual lesson.

4. The teacher of the televised lesson has had more time to prepare the lesson in all its details, with more care than would be possible in the daily lesson planning even of a teacher with equivalent skill and teaching ability, in the course of a day's routines.

5. All relevant visual aids may be assembled by the teacher-specialist working in advance of the televised lesson.

6. A school may provide for instruction in a language where no specialist is available, e.g., Russian.

DISADVANTAGES OF TV. Disadvantages of television in the classroom have often been pointed out:

1. The "personal" give-and-take of teacher and pupil are necessarily absent.

2. The lessons may not correlate with the rest of the work of the class.

3. The teacher may feel that he is being downgraded and made into merely an accessory to the lesson, or a tutor.

4. The school time schedule may not fit the announced television hour.

FOREIGN LANGUAGES AND TV

THE ABOVE ADVANTAGES and disadvantages apply to televised teaching generally, in all subject areas. We shall bring the question specifically to the area of foreign languages.

1. The teacher of the foreign language course may be a native speaker, and may bring "ideal" pronunciation into the language class.

2. Where pronunciation is involved, a televised "close-up" gives all students in the room the same opportunity to see the lips of the speaker, which is frequently of great help in imitating the sound. The teacher in the classroom is less visible to students at the back of the room than the televised teacher on the screen.

3. The television program may have been prepared by combining the best talents of a native speaker with those of an American-born or American-trained teacher, so that the theory and the presentation

may be the result of the combined specific skills of several members of the television teaching staff.

4. Since the sudden growth of interest in language study may in certain sections of the country create a situation in which language teachers may be assigned to teach languages in which they do not have conversational fluency, the televised presentation of foreign speech supplements the teacher's skill and permits the introduction of additional languages, such as Russian, which now is growing in popularity beyond the present capability of many schools to provide trained teachers with speaking competence.

The disadvantages of televised language programs may be overcome, as follows:

1. Some television programs show the teacher conducting a class on the screen. In such programs the student can identify himself with the studio class and share the reactions of those students to the teacher. If the situation is preserved as a natural one, the studio class will make typical erroneous as well as correct responses, and the observers will get the benefit of the teacher's instruction to the studio class.

2. Since the televised lessons will not constitute the entire course, but will generally be an enrichment or supplement, the regular teacher will provide the personal element in the other lessons.

3. Since the student of a language should have as great an amount of aural drill as possible, it will be an advantage to a class to view the program, whether or not the relationship to the rest of the course is very close. The ultimate aim of language instruction is to provide the student with language competence usable outside the schoolroom. The televised lesson provides an intermediate stage between the student's own classroom and an unstructured life situation where the foreign language is used.

4. Since the televised program may be viewed by groups larger than a single class, it becomes worth while to reschedule the language classes to permit several hundred students to view the program in an auditorium on certain days, and since the auditorium situation may permit the saving of teacher time, the students may meet in groups even smaller than the regular classes for the follow-up lessons which will provide the personal contact, the check on homework, and so on.

By integrating televised lessons with class lessons in foreign languages, the school may:

1. Add interest to the program by utilizing a new medium of instruction.

2. Bring additional personalities and different speech patterns into the language class.

3. Provide large-group televised instruction supplemented by small-group follow-up drill sessions, test sessions, or conference time.

4. Offer additional languages beyond the fluent conversational powers of the teachers on the staff—as, for example, Russian.

TELEVISION LEARNING INFORMAL. As in the case of the tape recorder and the language laboratory, the use of television in teaching has given new insights into learning, especially the learning of a foreign language. The learner sees an action going on; he is overwhelmed with a flood of strange sounds and sentences; gradually, by intuition and inference, certain meanings and expressions become clear to him. Through repetition his perception is increased and refined; at length he imitates. By constant practice he finally achieves a satisfactory level of performance.

This entire process is similar to that of a child learning the vernacular. A review of the elements involved in child learning will show how strikingly similar the two are. A child, outside of school, learns his mother tongue by these means:

1. Listening and hearing constantly.
2. Endless repetitions of useful expressions.
3. Trial and error, in his attempts to speak.
4. A high degree of motivation.
5. Being entirely unaware of such things as grammar and syntax.
6. Imitation.
7. The absence of a teacher who guides, selects, comments, and corrects.

As in the case of the language laboratory, the two basic principles involved are repetition on the part of the machine and imitation on the part of the pupil. The intellectual is minimized; acuity of perception, memory, and the power of imitation are relied upon. This opens up two possibilities with reference, first, to pupil clientele and, second, to the type of program to be presented.

MATERIALS AND TECHNIQUES

THE USE OF TELEVISION in teaching implies a radically different approach to learning. In the traditional classroom the teacher presents a certain body of subject matter, explains it, and applies it. There is some imitation in the language class, but in great part the intellectual faculties are exercised. On the basis of rules learned and reading selections read, the student tries to express simple ideas in the foreign language. One of the chief functions of the teacher is the correction of errors.

The lesson on the screen changes all this. The student listens almost exclusively, except for the brief reading of captions. Activity goes on continually; the spoken word is linked to the action. Practically all of the speech consists of conversation. There is extremely little in the way of exposition or narration. Grammar and syntax are rarely referred to, if mentioned at all.

To make learning effective, especially the learning of a language, expression must immediately follow impression. The participation of the learner consists of his repeating what he hears, at the urging of the TV teacher. ("Repita Vd. por favor. Otra vez, otra vez.")

The pupil's attention—we hope!—is riveted on the screen. If such is the case, a close intimate relationship is established between teacher and pupil. This feeling of proximity will, of course, depend on the effectiveness of the teacher and on the eagerness and interest of the pupil.

Since the material will consist largely of given speech patterns which are to be repeated, every effort must be made to make them attractive. Much repetition of trite material will lead to boredom. The material must be organized so that no word or expression is lost. After all, the pupil cannot say to the TV teacher, "I didn't hear what you said!"

Considerable reliance must be placed, too, on the ability of the pupil to evaluate his own performance. That is, is he aware of his mistakes? Can he correct them himself?

The TV Teacher. As has been indicated, in order to secure the participation of the learner, he must be induced to participate, otherwise television becomes but one-way communication. Now, since the TV teacher is unable to rouse or stimulate the individual pupil by a personal comment, he can reach the learner only by the power of suggestion. This means a skillful use of all the tricks of the actor: voice, gesture, facial expression, praise, joyful anticipation, satisfaction. The pupil must be so won over that his relationship to the figure on the screen is almost as close as to his living classroom teacher. One corollary of this is that the TV teacher not only should speak impeccably whatever language is being taught but should also possess an attractive personality, charm, and an ingratiating voice. We must remember that education is competing with entertainment and that our youngsters are accustomed to technical perfection in that field.

TV PROGRAM. So far, sad to relate, the competition has not been keen. In fact, many "educational" programs are dull. Their chief weakness is that they reproduce the classroom. Now, this is exactly what television should not do! Television should do for us what the ordinary classroom cannot do. We do not need a highly technical, costly instrument to show the pupil a strange teacher with a book, a blackboard (only part of one!), and a desk. For this purpose the average classroom, however modest in equipment, and the living teacher are far superior.

Again, television should do what the teacher cannot do. This is especially vital in the teaching of foreign languages. Here is a marvelous instrument offering wonderful possibilities which have not even been tapped. It is deplorable that in the United States, where the motion picture and television have reached their highest development, the educational program is so poor. Foreign languages can be taught on the screen but the programs must be vastly improved.

What can television do for the teaching of foreign languages?

Since action and speech are combined on the screen, television is ideal for presenting simultaneously the two most important facets of language learning—facility in speaking and acquaintance with the foreign culture. The TV program should afford practice in the foreign tongue in life situations in the foreign country.

This would seem almost obvious. However, up to date the average foreign language program presents a teacher standing before a blackboard, using chalk and charts, and moving in a purely classroom atmosphere. On a program for small children she may make use of dolls or toys. But there is no attempt to transfer the pupil from the classroom to the foreign country.

The scene in the foreign country need not be elaborate. We are not thinking of a bullfight or a chariot race! With a little ingenuity, however, and a few props (and a number of actors), the following scenes in the foreign country can be depicted:

1. The family at home.
2. The family at dinner.

3. Children playing ball.
4. Two students preparing their studies.
5. A telephone conversation.
6. A walk in the park.
7. At the zoo.
8. Buying a dress (shoes, tie, etc.).
9. At the restaurant.
10. A birthday party.
11. Mother awakens the lazy boy.
12. At the doctor's.
13. Preparing for a trip.
14. On the farm.
15. Christmas.

Effectiveness of TV with Young Children. In view of the major premises stated above, it is obvious that television is an excellent teaching device for young children. With much enthusiasm, but not too substantial results, the teaching of foreign languages to pupils in the grades has been undertaken in thousands of communities throughout the country. The chief weakness of FLES, as it is called, are:

1. Dearth of well-trained teachers.
2. Lack of agreement as to when to begin, length of period, extent of course, specific aims.
3. No uniformity or standards in materials.
4. Imperfect articulation with upper grades.
5. Difficulty of evaluation.
6. Cost.

At least four of the above problems can be solved by the use of television. Since an educational television program can be organized for an entire state, it will perforce be uniform and standardized for all the children within a given school system. Experts are utilized as teachers.

The program can be so set up that the teaching is done entirely on the screen. The classroom teacher is merely a proctor; he need not know a word of the foreign tongue in the beginning. By watching the program together with the children and repeating with them, the teacher will unconsciously acquire some facility. He should learn more quickly than the pupils; he will, if he once had French or Spanish or German at school or college. The learning situation can become a very interesting one, building up rapport between teacher and pupil.

Since the audio-visual method provides a more natural situation for learning a language, and since the process is one of imitation rather than cognition, it seems reasonable to suggest that not only bright children be admitted to language classes but that such instruction be more widely extended. Assuming that the child has no physical or mental defects, he should be able to profit from exposure to a foreign language.

One serious omission in the conventional educational program is the almost complete absence of music and song. Nothing will liven up the program more than a gay melody; nothing tops off the program more effectively than a song.

If the props are carefully selected and the acting is good, not only will the interest of the pupils be held but they will imbibe a great deal of culture quite unconsciously and informally. They will see the Parisian eating a *croissant* (possibly hear him munching it!); they will watch with delight the performance in costume of the *jarabe tapatia*. They will enjoy the singing of "Gaudeamus igitur" by the Heidelberg student; they will be eager to hop into a gondola and float down the Grand Canal.

The dialogue, the conversation, will be perfectly natural, for it will be that of a life situation. Pauses will be left for the observer to repeat; unobtrusively and gently he may be induced to say each phrase. On no account, however, should the teacher's voice command: "Repeat!" The classroom atmosphere should be nonexistent. In fact, the "teacher," as such, should be absent. In his place will be the leading actor, the "father," the "uncle," or the guide.

TV with or without the Teacher? There are two schools of thought with regard to the use of television in the classroom. One school would rely exclusively on the screen; the other would implement the TV program with drill and activities arranged by the live teacher. The former seems to be safer—if not more effective—wherever the classroom teacher is not qualified to teach a foreign language. On the other hand, where there is a classroom or a special teacher available who is competent in the foreign tongue, the class can benefit immensely by the extra practice provided. At this point all errors in the pupils' pronunciation can be corrected. Also, the follow-up provides an excellent opportunity for evaluating the pupils' achievement.

Television Program
(Spanish)
LA PUERTA ABIERTA

The New York State Board of Regents sponsors an Educational Television Project which includes two programs in Spanish given three times a week. The beginning lessons, presented at 10:20 A.M., are given by Mrs. Paul Glasgow; the advanced lessons at 1:30 P.M. are done by Professor Mary Finocchiaro of Hunter College. The programs are intended for children in grades 4 through 6. The advanced program is for those who have had a year of Spanish. The teachers have prepared the program and the manual.

Both TV teachers are young, attractive, and vivacious women who present a lively program. Their pronunciation is excellent. They make liberal use of charts, pictures, dolls, and toys. A great deal of interesting activity is crowded into these 20-minute programs.

Considerable reliance is placed on the classroom teacher. As the manual, reviewed by Paul M. Glaude, State Supervisor of Modern Languages, says:

> "It is she who must provide motivation. She may create interest by announcing the title of the program about to be presented. The children will enjoy trying to guess what the program will be about. The teacher will encourage the children to follow the directions of the studio teacher. She will watch the children's reactions and inform the studio teachers of needed help. If her school has a tape recorder, she will arrange with the principal for a transcription to be made of each program so that the tape can be played back at will for further listening."

The manual consists of a 30-page booklet which is designed to "guide the teacher's viewing of the programs as they are presented to her pupils. She is requested NOT to reproduce any part for distribution to children, nor should excerpts from the lessons be written on the chalkboard. To use the manual in these ways would nullify the aural-oral approach which is the essence of foreign language instruction for young children."

Television / 105

Unit I   Meeting New Friends

Program 1   Getting Acquainted   Mon., Sept. 21
Key Expressions   English
Buenos días, niños.   Good morning, children.
¿Cómo se llama usted?   What is your name?
Me llamo——.   My name is——.
Adiós.   Good-by.

Program 2   Where do they live?   Wed., Sept. 23
Key Expressions   English
Es una casa.   It's a house.
La casa es pequeña.   The house is small.
Hasta la vista.   Until I see you again.

Additional Vocabulary
una niña   a girl
un niño   a boy
mediana   middle-sized
grande   big
uno   one
dos   two
tres   three

Program 3   Our Friends Take a Bow   Fri., Sept. 25
Key Expressions   English
El señor Colón vive en la casa.   Mr. Colon lives in the house.

Additional Vocabulary
Perla   Pearl
Paco   Frank
Juanito   Johnny
Coco   Coco
Chato   "Pug-nose"
Pepito   Joey
cuatro   four
cinco   five
seis   six

Program 4   How Big Is the Family?   Mon., Sept. 28
Key Expressions   English
Hay seis personas en la familia   There are six people in the Co-
Colón.   lon family.
¿Cuántas personas hay en la fam-   How many are there in the Co-
ilia Colón?   lon family?

106

En mi familia hay seis personas.	In my family there are six people.
En su familia hay cuatro personas.	In your family there are four people.

Additional Vocabulary

siete	seven
ocho	eight
nueve	nine
diez	ten
once	eleven
doce	twelve

Television Program

(Spanish)

SPANISH THROUGH TELEVISION

In Public School 33 in the Chelsea district of New York the Harvard program "Spanish Through Television," designed by Christine Gibson, is presented three times weekly on a closed circuit. The only part the classroom teacher plays is to turn on the set for the lesson and then to turn it off at the end of the program. It is given from 9:30 to 10:00 in the morning. The children are to learn solely by watching the screen and repeating what they hear. A great part of the program consists of stick figures, such as those in the booklet *Spanish Through Pictures*. The child sees the picture, hears the voice, reads the caption, and repeats the expression.

The program is divided into six sections with a caption in Spanish (*Instrucciones, Explicación,* etc.) but the introductory voice in each case is in English. The Spanish voice or voices are those of natives. A typical program goes as follows:

Brief musical introduction. "Spanish Through Television" announced.

Instrucciones. Pupils instructed to repeat. Review of previous program. Stick figures portraying man seated in living room reading. Gets up to go to other room and get a book. Meanwhile the bird flies from the cage, the door of which has been left open. Conversation between man and wife about the bird that has flown.

Most captions are brief; some run to three lines being squeezed into the frame. Children are supposed to remember captions word for word, and to reproduce them for each picture as it is shown. Three tenses are employed: the present, the preterite, and the future, including those of irregular verbs like *salir, ser, ir,* etc.

Explicación. Instructions in English. New material. Pictures and voice; no captions. Pupils expected to memorize sentences as they are given. Class repeats each one in chorus.

Instrucciones. Two live persons appear on the screen: a young lady, an American tourist in Madrid, who asks a native where the Calle Mayor is. A conversation about stores and shopping ensues. Stress is placed on the future of *comprar.* Various articles in the shop are mentioned.

Stick figures appear. Father leaves; mother and children go shopping. Children repeat what Spanish voice says. No captions.

Repita. Same scene: mother going shopping with children, buys them new hats. Captions. Children repeat each one.

Explicación. Saleslady is shown in a shop. Counter with various garments; evidently Mexican. Saleslady talks about her merchandise. American tourist enters. Looks, asks, examines, makes purchase. Friend enters. More conversation. Bill added up. Both leave. Pupils listen.

Explicación. "Now test yourself . . ." The shopping scene of above with stick figures reappears. As each picture is shown, pupils are supposed to say the appropriate expression. These appear immediately thereafter as the caption for the picture. This exercise completes the lesson.

The instructions are that the class teacher is to have no part in the lesson and so, in this particular case, she sits at the side and watches —and learns—together with the pupils. The principal of the school, however, himself a former language teacher, concluded that the television program alone was inadequate and asked a Spanish-speaking (Puerto Rican) teacher to take the class after each showing. The additional oral practice seems to be quite effective. It at least serves the purpose of getting active pupil participation. At the end of the half hour of television some of the children appear to be a little bored. The entrance of the live teacher perks them up again.

THE LANGUAGE LABORATORY AT NEW YORK UNIVERSITY

[VII]

The Foreign Language Laboratory

WHAT IS A LANGUAGE LABORATORY?

THE LANGUAGE LABORATORY is the most important techno-
logical aid to language teaching. Although certain basic considerations are involved, there is considerable variety in the
equipment of the laboratory. It may range all the way from one
machine with earphones on open desks or tables for a half dozen
students, to forty or fifty booths, each equipped with tape recorder,
earphones and control buttons.

Stated in its simplest terms, a language laboratory is a special
room with electronic equipment set aside for language practice by
students. The tape recorder alone, as used by the teacher, does not
constitute a laboratory. The distinctive feature is the possibility of
practice by the learner. Although this is usually done in a room set
aside for that purpose, the ordinary classroom can be transformed

into a lab momentarily during the classroom period, or after school hours, if it has the necessary apparatus.

As stated above, the laboratory is an "aid" to language teaching. It does not take over the whole procedure nor does it replace the teacher. It need not even be considered the central factor in language teaching, although there are language specialists who would say that it is. The most widely accepted point of view is that the language lesson is initiated and developed in the classroom; it is expanded and practiced in the lab.

The notion that the laboratory can replace the teacher is entirely false. It cannot take the teacher's place or make up for any weaknesses on his part. In fact, it is of no advantage for the weak or inexperienced teacher. Actually, it demands a well trained and an intelligent teacher to make the most effective use of the equipment. The poorer teacher will bungle the work in the lab; he will be more effective without it.

There are two basic factors which make it possible for the lab, when properly used, to greatly increase the effectiveness of the classroom teacher. The first is that the student will hear native voices of different kinds, speaking at normal, everyday speed. In the traditional classroom the student hears only the voice of his teacher, who is usually not a native speaker.

The second strength of the laboratory is that it provides the possibility of almost unlimited practice outside the classroom. As we all know, the mastery of a foreign language depends upon constant and unceasing practice. Under ordinary school conditions the student sits in a classroom five times a week; he may be called upon to recite once or twice each time. One teacher who kept a record of the time devoted to oral recitation found that it amounted to 87 minutes per student for a term. In the lab the student can produce orally for an entire period. The mechanical equipment makes it possible for the teacher to supervise, to check and to monitor his oral production. The instructor listens in and corrects the errors of the learner.

The claim has been made by some enthusiasts that the laboratory greatly relieves the teacher of much drudgery. This is not quite true. Physically there is some relief; the teacher can save his voice, for he will be heard even if he speaks softly through the microphone. Also, if the students are given appropriate materials for practice, he need only monitor much of the time.

The crux of the matter, however, is the production of the appropriate materials. There are many commercially prepared tapes on the market and most basic textbooks now come equipped with tapes and pattern drills. But in addition to this the teacher will continually be called upon to prepare extra tapes, special drills and timely spoken selections. This requires a good deal of time and effort. In some cases it has been found that it takes fifteen hours of preparation for one hour of demonstration. In fact, lab materials require more time and care than other teaching materials, for they must not only be clear but also graded, varied, interesting and linked up with the textbook and the daily lesson.

AIMS OF THE LABORATORY

THE USE OF the language laboratory is based on the notion that understanding and speaking are the prime essentials in acquiring a foreign language. Since we learn what we do, extensive and systematic practice in hearing and speaking is necessary. Inasmuch as the conventional classroom does not make sufficient provision for such practice, resort must be had to another device. That is the language laboratory.

The fundamental aim, then, of the laboratory is to provide much and regular practice in listening to models, in imitating these models and in repetitive oral drills. Constant listening will build up the ability to understand the foreign language. Oral drills will strengthen the ability to speak fluently. The chief advantage of the use of the language laboratory is the fact that it provides practice in the spoken language.

SPEAKING IS ABSOLUTELY ESSENTIAL. Practically all modern language teachers are now agreed that the grammar-translation and reading methods are outmoded and that the aural-oral objective is the most desirable one in learning a language.

It is well, however, to avoid extremes. With reference to the psychology of language learning the following facts must be pointed out:

1. Language, it is true, is primarily speech. The very words for language—langue, lengua, lingua—mean "tongue." Every language, however, except the most primitive, has a written form. Learning to read is a phase of language study; writing follows almost immediately.

2. Aside from multiple sense appeal, there is a close psychological relationship between the different phases of language learning. They cannot be separated.

3. The protagonists of the reading aim were right when they claimed that it was easier for the teacher and the student, and was more lasting. Rapid comprehension of the spoken language is a far more difficult skill. And so is fluent and accurate speech.

4. For the student, and particularly for the adult learner, a knowledge of grammatical structure is important. More important, however, is actual practice in hearing and speaking the language.

5. Language mastery demands the development of habits of automatic response. This can be achieved only by frequent, highly motivated drill exercises and much repetition.

The language laboratory, then, can accomplish that which the ordinary classroom cannot. The use of orthophonic devices increases the quality and the quantity of the student's performance.

THE TEACHER AND THE LANGUAGE LABORATORY

ALTHOUGH THE MACHINE cannot replace the teacher, it actually increases the teacher's usefulness in the following ways:

1. Since the teacher is linked by means of the headphones to every student, she has a much closer individual relationship. It is her voice alone which the student hears; she commands complete attention.

2. Since the student's activity is practically uninterrupted, his attention is fully engaged, his interest is held, and he is highly motivated. The teacher deals with a group in which everyone is participating eagerly.

3. Instruction is really individualized in the most practical way, for there is an intimate, private interchange between teacher and learner.

4. Because of this privacy, the student is not embarrassed when he makes errors. His classmates do not hear them, only the teacher who is there to help and guide, as well as to correct.

5. The teacher can build up certain qualities which are largely lost in the conventional classroom, namely, self-evaluation and self-criticism on the part of the student.

ADVANTAGES OF THE LANGUAGE LABORATORY. The use of orthophonic devices aids language learning in the following ways:

1. Practically all of the objectives of a language course can be achieved in the laboratory: speaking, understanding, pronouncing, learning vocabulary, carrying on a conversation, memorizing, reading, and dictation.

2. The near-ideal pronunciation of native speakers is always available in the laboratory.

3. The student becomes readily accustomed to different kinds of voices—male and female, old and young, coarse and fine, etc. In the conventional classroom he hears only his teacher's voice.

4. In the laboratory the student can listen over and over again. "Repetitio mater studiorum."

5. The laboratory gives every student an opportunity to practice individually during the whole period. In the classroom he generally recites or speaks but a few minutes at each session.

6. The devices in the laboratory allow for immediate correction. The student can compare his performance at once with the master record. The teacher can identify habitual errors by listening to the student's recording.

7. The laboratory relieves the teacher of many tasks, such as dictation.

8. By constant repetition and oral drill the student acquires with ease a new set of speech habits—the real objective of learning a foreign language.

LIMITATIONS OF THE LABORATORY. As has been pointed out before, every mechanical device for learning has its advantages and its disadvantages. In the case of the language laboratory the chief danger is that the procedures may become monotonous. If the student's alertness is not maintained, he will become drowsy and only half listen to what is being said. Monotony may be avoided by:

1. Avoiding the use of lengthy recordings.

2. Introducing musical selections.

3. Providing much opportunity for student participation. This can be done by allowing pauses in the tapes or records for the student to repeat. It can also be done by letting the student record his voice on the record or tape.

4. Variety not only is the spice of life but the spice of the lesson. No single exercise should be used too long.

5. The use of frequent lively dialogues with several voices and dramatic action will help to maintain interest.

6. Providing opportunities for the student to express himself in original material in the foreign language.

TYPES OF LANGUAGE LABORATORIES

As STATED BEFORE, the language laboratory may range all the way from a few simple mechanical devices to the latest complex orthophonic installation. The less pretentious setup usually provides only for listening and thus does not secure the optimum values of the laboratory idea. It is only where the microphone and recording device are included that the oral as well as the aural aim is achieved.

KINDS OF INSTALLATIONS. The various types of installations may be classified on different bases. There is the classroom with fixed machines, used only part-time by the foreign language classes. The equipment may be installed in the desks; it is locked up when not in use. Or, the equipment is kept in a storage room or closet, and is wheeled in on "wagons" when needed. Both types of installation, of course, impose serious limitations.

The true laboratory consists of a separate room, specifically designed to contain the equipment and used only for language practice. In the case of the special laboratory there are essentially two varieties. The first type consists of centrally controlled recording and playback machines from which the sound is sent by wire to each student at his position. There may be several machines with different programs given simultaneously.

The second type of installation consists of booths in each of which there is a recorder-player controlled by the student himself. The two types may be combined, of course.

THE CLASSROOM INSTALLATION. A normal classroom is equipped with a certain number of audio-visual devices, controlled by the teacher. Each student at his desk is provided with earphones. The phonograph, tape recorder, and microphone will be in the front of the room. There may also be a screen and a motion-picture projector, as well as a filmstrip projector. The room should, of course, be provided with shades so that it may be darkened when required.

This is rather simple and inexpensive equipment. The great advantage of having it in the regular language room is that the use of the mechanical aids can be readily integrated with the various aspects of the lesson. If the school can provide only one room of this type, it may be considered the laboratory. It will then be used once or twice a week by each foreign language class. More ideal is the equipment of every foreign language classroom with a complete set of audio-visual devices.

THE MOBILE INSTALLATION. Because of the expense, the lack of space, and the school program, it may be advisable to employ mobile units. A certain number of "wagons"—that is, tables on wheels—will be equipped with small soundproof partitions containing a playback machine, a microphone, and a tape recorder. When needed, these five or six wagons are wheeled into the front or the rear of the classroom. It may be necessary to remove a row of desks to provide room for them. These machines will then be used, in succession, by a given number of pupils while the rest of the class is engaged in another activity. Each wagon is wired and is connected with a central panel controlled by the teacher. Or, the choice is left to the student; he turns on the tape or disc that he wishes, or is instructed, to hear.

THE LISTENING LAB. One step closer to the real language laboratory is the listening room. It may be provided with sufficient listening posts for an entire class. If it is installed in the lounge or the library, the use of earphones will prevent disturbing other students. To secure the optimum advantages of the listening room there should be in charge a teacher or monitor who is ready to distribute records or tapes as requested. Students will come to the room for extra practice before and after school, or in their free periods.

THE PRACTICE ROOM. Facilities for listening and reviewing may vary all the way from an alcove or a longer table in a given office to a special room provided with an elaborate panel and monitors to check on the students. The smaller accommodations will be reserved for individual students and smaller groups. If a separate room is available, it can be used by an entire class.

As will be seen from the above, the types of organization fall into two categories: the modified classroom and the separate room. Strictly speaking, only the latter can be considered a true language laboratory.

The Language Laboratory /

SUPERVISION. If optimum results are to be attained, careful supervision must be provided. This will be both technical and pedagogical. The machines will have to be kept in good condition. Occasionally, servicing will be necessary. Mischievous tampering on the part of the students must be prevented.

The pedagogic aspect includes the supervision and checking of the students' practice, the organizing of the drills, the preparation of programs, the distribution of materials, the assigning of extra practice, etc.

TECHNICAL CONSIDERATIONS IN CONNECTION WITH THE LABORATORY

IN VIEW OF THE FACT that every sound should be heard clearly, it is imperative that the language laboratory be located in the quietest part of the building. It certainly should not face a street that is noisy or a playground that is used during the school day.

For the sake of efficiency and economy the laboratory should be located near the foreign language classes and not too far from the foreign language office.

The room should be so soundproofed that both reverberations and outside noises are at a minimum. In this connection the doors and the windows should be given special consideration. The structure of the room should be carefully planned with reference to acoustics.

Considerable heat is generated by electronic devices. It is therefore necessary to plan for adequate ventilation, possibly air conditioning. The windows should be provided with Venetian blinds. The electric illumination should be such that it does not interfere with the electronic devices.

It is important, too, that the interior of the booths be treated so that much of the sound of the occupant's voice is absorbed.

Employing Laboratory Techniques in the Classroom. Since the language laboratory is so new and since it will take a long time before all schools are equipped with one, it is profitable to consider what audial techniques the average teacher can employ in the traditional classroom. It will mean essentially a transfer in stress from visual to aural learning.

Traditionally, of course, the book is the basic source of subject matter and the visual appeal has necessarily been the accepted mode of learning. Even auditory correctness was based on visual presentation, through phonetic symbols, which are a visual index to correct pronunciation.

The language record and tape have made listening a practical classroom experience. The tape recorder should be part of the equipment of every progressive teacher of a foreign language. A single hearing of a foreign word or sentence is insufficient for learning. The tape recorder makes it possible to repeat any number of times without the slightest variation in pronunciation.

Ear-training practice should be included in every lesson. The tape is the most convenient device for ensuring the complete identity of material. Ease of recording and of erasure makes the preparation of audial materials no more difficult than mimeographing. For the sake of economy teachers in the same department may exchange their tapes.

The use of taped materials makes it possible to give the class the experience of hearing other voices than that of the teacher. The average student, trained in the traditional classroom, is so accustomed to one voice that often he is mystified when another teacher or a stranger speaks. The systematic use of the tape recorder overcomes this difficulty in time. It prepares the student for easy comprehension of foreign voices on the radio or on a sound film.

THE STUDENT IN THE LABORATORY. Basically the foreign language laboratory is a room equipped with machines which act as absolutely reliable, patient, and tireless tutors. With unvarying fidelity they are ready by the turn of a lever to reproduce sounds and sentences at any time of the day and for any length of time. In other words, they are able to provide endless experience in hearing and speaking—the two basic language skills. The advantages of the laboratory in promoting learning are obvious:

1. With the mechanical equipment every pupil is able to get active language practice throughout the period. In a traditional classroom of forty students with a 40-minute period, even if the lesson is well organized, each student gets only about a half minute in which to recite.

2. In the traditional classroom each student advances at the same pace. Each one must cover the same amount of material; there is little possibility for differentiation. In the language laboratory, however, it is possible to provide for different levels of learning and to adjust the rate of progress to the capacity of the learner.

3. Teachers are human beings. At the end of the day they are tired, if not completely exhausted. A machine does not tire. Hence, the student can get much additional practice by making use of the laboratory in free periods and after regular school hours. The laboratory provides that additional practice which is so necessary for efficient language learning.

4. In the traditional classroom even the most alert and progressive teacher is tempted to have daily and continual resort to the textbook. The students expect it. The laboratory makes the audial approach easy and natural. The student hears the language before he sees its written forms.

5. In the laboratory the student is face to face with something impersonal and thus loses all feeling of self-consciousness. Those qualities and acts of the teacher which may produce an unpleasant reaction on the part of the student, such as impatience, sarcasm, critical comments, and the giving of a grade, are absent. The removal of inhibitions actually improves the oral facility of the learner.

6. If the tapes have been prepared by cultured native speakers, the student can listen to perfect models. Even if the American teacher is well trained, he will not in all cases give the nuances and intonation to his speech which the native uses.

PROBLEMS IN CONNECTION WITH THE USE OF THE LABORATORY. Despite its many advantages, the laboratory does not solve all problems in the teaching of foreign languages. Since it is, after all, but a collection of machines, it cannot replace the teacher, the human being. It can be a very effective aid, but it is and must remain an auxiliary device. Some of the problems that present themselves with reference to the language laboratory are:

1. The mechanical equipment of the laboratory may be almost perfect but it will not be effective if the materials are not good. Care must be exercised in choosing tapes, recordings, and films.

2. Granted that the equipment is superior and the materials are excellent, there still remains the use to which they are put by the teacher. Audio-visual aids are quite new to most teachers. How can they be trained so that they will use the aids effectively?

3. There is a considerable variety of types of installations. Which one is a given school to choose? Which type is best for the elementary school, the junior high school, the high school, and the college?

4. To what extent can equipment and materials be used at home for extra practice?

5. What arrangements have to be made to take care of the laboratory mechanically and pedagogically? To what extent may monitors and technicians be used? What additional expense does this entail?

THE EFFECTIVENESS OF ORTHOPHONIC DEVICES

ALTHOUGH CLASS INSTRUCTION IS UNIVERSALLY PREVALENT and its socializing phases have been highly praised, the ideal learning situation is probably that of one teacher for each student. That is, of course, entirely out of the question under normal conditions. Audial devices have, however, made this quite possible, even in a classroom of forty students. Mechanical aids make possible what is an almost ideal situation for learning a language in school, namely:

1. Hearing is stressed. Since language is basically sound, the sense of hearing must be appealed to more than any other. In fact, authorities insist that hearing should occupy 40 per cent of the time. Speaking should be given 30 per cent; reading 20, and writing only 10 per cent.

2. The learner is isolated. He is removed from the distracting influences of his classmates. He is occupied solely with himself and with his task of learning. He can proceed at his own pace.

3. The learner is brought as close as possible to the speaker—either his teacher or the native voice on the tape or record.

In the normal classroom the learner is continually distracted by sights and sounds not related to the matter in hand. The use of earphones eliminates extraneous sounds; being seated in a booth shuts out distracting sights. The student hears only the teacher's voice. The microphone provides the opportunity for him to speak and to imitate his teacher's voice. Both voices can be heard through the earphones. Thus, the pupil and the teacher are alone and his entire attention is concentrated on his own listening and responding.

It is also possible to record both voices on one tape. The teacher's voice is recorded on the master channel and the learner's voice on the lower channel. The tape may be rewound and then the student can hear both channels. This gives him an opportunity to compare his performance with that of the teacher. The student can erase his own recording and try again. This can be done any number of times, until the student feels that his performance is nearly perfect.

Since his own voice is fed to his ears electronically, his hearing is much keener. The model voice, too, reaches him clearly and without interference. It has been found that the speed of learning a foreign language has been greatly increased by the use of orthophonic devices. It varies from 30 to 80 per cent.

HOW THE LANGUAGE LAB IS USED

ORIGINAL TAPES. The language laboratory in Sheepshead Bay (N.Y.) High School is provided with 14 booths and 21 listening stations. The students at the latter are called "listeners." The fourteen in the booth with microphones are referred to as "speakers."

The two French 4 classes use the laboratory twice a week for planned instruction. The other foreign language classes are invited for more or less informal activities.

The following procedures are employed:

1. The entire class listens to a recording, for the purpose of comprehension and aural practice. This is done for 3–4 minutes.

2. A pronunciation drill of the same length of time. The "speakers" pronounce words and expressions at the microphone. They hear themselves through earphones. The 21 "listeners" meanwhile repeat silently or softly.

3. A tape is put on which provides drill on some grammatical point or which consists of questions and answers. For example, a pattern drill may be given involving the *passé composé*. This works out as follows:

Teacher's voice on tape:	je parle
Student repeats:	je parle
Student says:	j'ai parlé
Teacher's voice:	j'ai parlé
Student repeats:	j'ai parlé

In other words, there are three student responses. The tape records them; the tape is rewound and played back. The student hears his own performance and compares it with the model.

In the meantime, the 21 "listeners" do the same exercise on paper. That is, instead of saying the verb form, they write it. At length the papers are collected, to be marked.

4. A variant of this procedure is as follows: The 21 listeners frequently finish first. The teacher then channels to the 21 listening stations the work of the "speakers" in the booths.

Since the teacher can communicate with the students he may interject comments.

5. The booth, of course, isolates the individual student. This has its advantages and disadvantages for learning. However, since language is basically for communication, exercises to give practice in this skill are arranged. For example, the speaker in booth A carries on a dialogue with the speaker in booth B. Meanwhile, the class listens. The teacher is in control; he makes corrections.

6. Sometimes songs are played and the entire class joins in the singing.

7. Occasionally, a dictation is given. Aside from the concentration of attention, no special advantage is gained by doing this in the laboratory.

By and large, the tapes used in the laboratory do not follow the textbook. The teacher prepares original material designed to give additional drill, paralleling the exercises in the book.

TAPES BASED ON TEXTBOOK. The method employed in the high schools of Montgomery County, Maryland, as described in Bulletin No. 3 of the Office of Education, is as follows (pp. 48–49):

"At the present time, the content of the tapes is prepared from the lessons in the textbooks in use in the various language classes. The procedure is as follows:

1. By way of preparation the teacher records the reading selection in the lesson at normal tempo.

2. He then reads the same passage in breath groups allowing ample pause for repetition by the entire class.

3. This exercise is replayed several times that day and each day thereafter until the entire lesson has been drilled adequately.

4. On the second day simple questions on the content, devised by the teacher, are added to the preceding exercises. They require on the part of the students almost a parroting of the phrases which they have heard in the reading selection and which they have repeated so frequently.

5. The following day the questions contained in the text—they are more difficult and constitute a part of the assignment of the

previous day—are played on the tape and the appropriate intervals allowed for the responses by the students.

"Whenever questions are asked, following the pause allowed for response by the students, the teacher's voice is heard giving the patterned response, and again an interval is allowed for repetition by the students. Verb drills and grammar drills are also taped. Dictation is advantageously administered by the tape, for in this situation there is a minimum of distraction, and the necessity of looking up from the paper at a speaker is obviated. It has been observed that the speed of writing approximates that which prevails when the students are writing their native language.

"The advantages of this method appear to be many. Every child has an opportunity to speak the language every day. Too, the method allows for individual correction. The teacher passes up and down the aisles, listening carefully and stopping to correct an individual student without interrupting those who are proceeding satisfactorily. This kind of controlled repetition and hearing makes for greater spontaneity of response. Tapes are made and/or provided containing the voices of native speakers, thus offering opportunities to hear the language as it is spoken. It is an excellent device for rectifying deficiencies due to absence, and for remedial work. As familiarity with the equipment progresses and the ingenuity of the teacher has time to function, it is to be hoped that the two skills of hearing and speaking a foreign language will be as effectively acquired as those of reading and writing a foreign language have been in the past."

USE OF THE FILM IN THE LABORATORY. Bulletin No. 3 of the Office of Education also describes the use of a sound film at Otterbein College:

> Its purpose is not motivation, enrichment, entertainment, or any other auxiliary function, but a language teaching film, an audio-visual text instead of a printed one. The film consists of a series of conversational episodes occurring in France. Two main characters carry the story and lead the student to identify himself with real personalities and actual situations in the foreign culture. The lip-synchronized conversational text is based on carefully graded vocabulary and syntactical items. No written text is used until the student can comprehend and use the language of a specific unit. The teaching procedure, in brief, is as follows:

In the classroom the student views the film repeatedly, getting from the situation and the conversation an understanding of the scene. He is led by the teacher, step by step, to figure out the relationship between sound and action. The sound then becomes identified with meaningful experience.

The student is given immediate oral drill on the language he has just comprehended. The material which is thus partially taught with the movie in the classroom becomes aural-oral homework on records in the laboratory. Plans are being developed for projectors to be used in the laboratory to continue the visual simultaneously with the aural-oral drill. Students must go to the laboratory to prepare this homework, since it is available nowhere else. Later the language patterns are practiced in a freer type of conversational situation, stimulated by the use of slides and still pictures. At this more creative stage the class is divided into small conversational units of 6 to 8 who are led by an advanced student in the language or by foreign-born departmental assistants and teachers.

When the student has sufficient aural-oral facility, he is taught to spell and then to read and to write. Grammar is taught as such only after the grammatical forms have already been learned in context and used meaningfully. An irregular verb is introduced in context when logically needed and always as a vocabulary item. More formal analysis and drill are given after students can use the verbs with comparative ease.

It has been found effective to combine sound, color, and teaching films with tape-recorded scripts and exercises. A story may be presented as follows:

The class hour, or part of it, can most profitably be devoted to providing the experience, telling the story with the visual support which assures its being understood and makes of it a real experience. This experience gives the student a frame of reference, a context in which vocabulary items find their place by association. Study, in the traditional sense of "learning words and rules," ceases to exist. Study becomes the repetition of speech in a known context, based on experience. . . . Meaning is best gathered and remembered from the oral and visual context as it is given in the taped dramatization and the accompanying slides. Listening to the tapes repeatedly conveys the meaning of practically every word. The situation created by the story, and the pictures, together with the intonation and voice qualifiers of the actors, interpret meaning.

Taken from Theodore Mueller and George Borglum, *Linguistic Pattern Practice Based on Saint-Exupéry's Le Petit Prince*. Foreign Language Department, University of Florida, Gainesville, 1958. Quoted on page 53 of Bulletin No. 3, U.S. Office of Education.

Suggestions for Successful Recording. Homemade tapes are not always effective, due to the lack of experience of the teacher. In fact, the poor results are almost wholly due to the human factor, for the machine rarely fails. To avoid inadequacies the following suggestions should prove helpful to the teacher:

1. Before attempting to make any recording, the teacher should check the equipment and make sure that it is in perfect condition.

2. The recording should be prepared in a quiet, sound-proof room, free from interruptions. In order to make the recording as perfect as possible, all extraneous sounds, as for instance, the rattling of paper, should be avoided.

3. The teacher should speak in a natural, relaxed manner; the subject should be presented with warmth and interest. Nothing is more deadly than a monotonous, dull and uninspiring production. In order to prevent pauses, omissions and corrections, it is highly recommended that the teacher be quite familiar with the material.

4. Instructions to the student should be simple and succinct. They may be in English, although, especially in advanced classes, it is preferable to give them in the foreign language.

5. The pauses for the student response should be timed with care. Frequently they are too long. The pause should not be so short that the student is unable to complete his answer, nor so long that he has to wait for the next item. Since the student response is much slower than that of the teacher, the latter should repeat the answer silently two or three times.

6. Voice quality is very important. As stated above, the teacher's voice should manifest warmth and interest in connected material. In detached sentences and drills the volume and tone should remain unchanged. To secure the correct volume, the microphone should be placed at the side of the mouth and at an even distance (about six inches, if crystal microphones are used). If it is placed too close to the mouth, the sound of breathing and the hiss of the sibilants may interefere.

7. It is advisable to play back the recording, to detect any errors or flaws.

8. After its first use in the laboratory, the teacher will be able to determine how effective the recording is. By checking carefully the teacher will be able to tell whether the material is too difficult or too easy, too long or too short, and whether the tempo at which it is uttered is too fast or too slow.

MATERIALS THAT CAN BE USED IN THE LABORATORY

ALTHOUGH the language laboratory is primarily set up for listening, every phase of language learning can be practiced effectively.

PRONUNCIATION AND INTONATION. By continually hearing the foreign sounds and repeating them, the pupil acquires correct pronunciation and intonation. If he records what he says, the pupil may compare his production with the original on the tape. In this way mispronunciations may be corrected and intonations improved. Special material designed for pronunciation practice may be placed on tapes with appropriate pauses for pupils to repeat and to record their imitation of the model. Good pronunciation may also be developed by reciting passages of prose and poetry, which may be memorized in the laboratory after being heard a number of times. The same is true of dialogues and of songs. The sequence for pronunciation is always listen and then repeat. The exercises should be so arranged that the pupil speaks, hears the correct form and then repeats the latter.

DRILLS IN FORMS AND STRUCTURES. In using exercises in which the pupil is to answer questions, add vocabulary or make a change in structure, the following principles are basic:
1. The pause must be long enough for the pupil to make the required insertion, answer or change.
2. The correct form must be given on the tape.
3. Enough time must be allowed for the pupil to repeat the correct form given on the tape model.

Structures may be drilled by using any of the ordinary pattern drills, except that no more than one basic change be involved in each unit. In the repetition drills, only listen-repeat is necessary. In changes in form the order is listen-change-listen-repeat.

Structure Drill
(Spanish)
GUSTAR

Cued responses. Student supplies indirect object pronoun.
Teacher: ¿Le gusta Vd. esta película? (*Pause*).
Student: Sí, me gusta.
Teacher: ¿Les gusta a los alumnos esta lección? (*Pause*).
Student: Sí, les gusta.
Teacher: ¿Nos gusta a nosotros este coche? (*Pause*).
Student: Sí, nos gusta.
Teacher: ¿Le gusta a él estas corbatas? (*Pause*).
Student: Sí, le gustan.
Teacher: ¿Le gusta a María esta falda? (*Pause*).
Student: Sí, le gusta.

Agreement of Adjectives

Teacher: Estamos en una tienda. Vd. compra varios artículos. ¿Desea Vd. una camisa roja? (*Pause*).
Student: Sí, deseo una camisa roja.
Teacher: ¿Pañuelo? (*Pause*).
Student: Sí, deseo un pañuelo rojo.
Teacher: ¿Corbatas? (*Pause*).
Student: Sí, deseo corbatas rojas.
Teacher: ¿Calcetines? (*Pause*).
Student: Sí, deseo calcetines rojos.
Teacher: ¿Pañuelos y corbatas? (*Pause*).
Student: Sí, deseo pañuelos y corbatas rojos.

Response Drill
(German)
Adjectives

Pupil chooses first adjective in each case.
Teacher: Haben Sie einen kleinen oder einen grossen Kugelschreiber verloren? (*Pause*).
Student: Ich habe einen kleinen Kugelschreiber verloren.
Teacher: Ich habe einen kleinen Kugelschreiber verloren. (*Pause*).
Student: Ich habe einen kleinen Kugelschreiber verloren.
Teacher: Haben Sie einen neuen oder einen alten Kugelschreiber gefunden? (*Pause*).

Student: Ich habe einen neuen Kugelschreiber gefunden.
Teacher: Ich habe einen neuen Kugelschreiber gefunden. (*Pause*).
Student: Ich habe einen neuen Kugelschreiber gefunden.
Teacher: Haben Sie mit einem schweren oder einem leichten Kugelschreiber geschrieben? (*Pause*).
Student: Ich habe mit einem schweren Kugelschreiber geschrieben.
Teacher: Ich habe mit einem schweren Kugelschreiber geschrieben. (*Pause*).
Student: Ich habe mit einem schweren Kugelschreiber geschrieben.
Teacher: Haben Sie einen blauen oder einen roten Kugelschreiber gekauft? (*Pause*).
Student: Ich habe einen blauen Kugelschreiber gekauft.
Teacher: Ich habe einen blauen Kugelschreiber gekauft. (*Pause*).
Student: Ich habe einen blauen Kugelschreiber gekauft.

AUDITORY COMPREHENSION. The greatest effectiveness of the laboratory undoubtedly is in the practice of aural comprehension, which is also the most interesting exercise to be put on tapes. Anecdotes, poems, prose passages, dialogues and conversation may be used. A direct connection with the classroom lesson can be made by taping selections from the textbook used by the class. In fact, if prepared with some skill, the comprehension lesson may involve practice in pronunciation, the learning of new vocabulary, answering questions on content (reading comprehension) and even a dictation exercise.

Several examples of taped laboratory exercises are given below.

ILLUSTRATIVE LESSONS
Laboratory Exercise
(French)
MAUPASSANT'S "LA FICELLE"

1. *Vocabulary. Here are some of the words and expressions used in this story. You will also hear the English translation. Do not repeat it. Repeat only the French words in the appropriate pauses.*
économe—thrifty—économe (*Pause*).
au milieu de—in the middle of—au milieu de (*Pause*).
insignifiant—insignificant—insignifiant (*Pause*).
la ficelle—the piece of string—la ficelle (*Pause*).
subitement—suddenly—subitement (*Pause*).
honteux—ashamed—honteux (*Pause*).
la poussière—dust—la poussière (*Pause*).

une idée fixe—a fixed idea—une idée fixe (*Pause*).

par terre—on the ground—par terre (*Pause*).

se moquer de—to make fun of—se moquer de (*Pause*).

le portefeuille—wallet—le portefeuille (*Pause*).

le passant—the passerby—le passant (*Pause*).

2. *Commençons la lecture (Read entire story at regular speed).*

3. *Vocabulary drill. Listen to the word or phrase as it is spoken, as it is used in a sentence, and as spoken again. Then write the word or phrase in French.*

économe—Le paysan normand est très économe.—économe (*Pause*).

insignifiant—Il ramasse les choses les plus insignifiantes.—insignifiant (*Pause*).

au milieu de—Il s'arrête au milieu de la route.—au milieu de (*Pause*).

la ficelle—Il met la ficelle dans sa poche.—la ficelle (*Pause*).

subitement—Subitement la police arrive.—subitement (*Pause*).

honteux—Ils ne sont pas honteux d'être injustes.—honteux (*Pause*).

la poussière—Il le trouve sur son chemin dans la poussière.—la poussière (*Pause*).

une idée fixe—Son idée fixe le rend malade.—une idée fixe (*Pause*).

par terre—Il regarde toujours par terre.—par terre (*Pause*).

se moquer de—Tout le monde se moque de lui.—se moquer de (*Pause*).

le portefeuille—Cet autre individu a rapporté le portefeuille.—le portefeuille (*Pause*).

le passant—Tout les passants secouent la tête et se moquent de lui.—le passant (*Pause*).

4. *Spaced reading. Let us go back to page 23, line 8. Beginning with "Un jour il va au marché," repeat what you hear in the appropriate pauses.*

5. *Questionnaire, p. 25. Answer the following questions, in French, in the first pause. Then you will be given the correct answer. Repeat it in the second pause.*

Teacher: Qui est Hauchecorne? (*Pause*).

Student: Hauchecorne est un paysan normand.

Teacher: Hauchecorne est un paysan normand. (*Pause*).

Student: Hauchecorne est un paysan normand.

Teacher: Qu'est-ce qui caractérise les Normands? (*Pause*).

Student: Les Normands sont très économes.

Teacher: Les Normands sont très économes. (*Pause*).

Student: Les Normands sont très économes.

Teacher: Où va Hauchecorne? (*Pause*).

Student: Il va au marché de Goderville.

Teacher: Il va au marché de Goderville. (*Pause*).

Student: Il va au marché de Goderville.

Teacher: Que ramasse-t-il en route? (*Pause*).

Student: Il ramasse une ficelle en route.

Teacher: Il ramasse une ficelle en route. (*Pause*).

Student: Il ramasse une ficelle en route.

Teacher: Qui aperçoit-il? (*Pause*).

Student: Il aperçoit Malandain, son ennemi.

Teacher: Il aperçoit Malandain, son ennemi. (*Pause*).

Student: Il aperçoit Malandain, son ennemi.

Teacher: Qu'est-ce qu'on apprend quelques heures plus tard? (*Pause*).

Student: On apprend qu'un portefeuille avec de l'argent a été perdu sur la route de Goderville.

Teacher: On apprend qu'un portefeuille avec de l'argent a été perdu sur la route de Goderville. (*Pause*).

Student: On apprend qu'un portefeuille avec de l'argent a été perdu sur la route de Goderville.

Teacher: Qui demande-t-on à l'auberge? (*Pause*).

Student: On demande Hauchecorne.

Teacher: On demande Hauchecorne. (*Pause*).

Student: On demande Hauchecorne.

Teacher: Qu'est-ce qu'on lui demande à la mairie? (*Pause*).

Student: On lui demande s'il a trouvé le portefeuille perdu.

Teacher: On lui demande s'il a trouvé le portefeuille perdu. (*Pause*).

Student: On lui demande s'il a trouvé le portefeuille perdu.

Teacher: Quelle réponse fait-il? (*Pause*).

Student: Il dit que ce n'était qu'une ficelle.

Teacher: Il dit que ce n'était qu'une ficelle. (*Pause*).

Student: Il dit que ce n'était qu'une ficelle.

Teacher: Pourquoi ne peut-il plus être accusé par la justice? (*Pause*).

Student: Un homme rapporte l'objet perdu.

Teacher: Un homme rapporte l'objet perdu. (*Pause*).

Student: Un homme rapporte l'objet perdu.

Teacher: Pourquoi les gens sourient-ils? (*Pause*).

Student: Ils pensent qu'il a donné le portefeuille à l'autre individu pour le rapporter.

Teacher: Ils pensent qu'il a donné le portefeuille à l'autre individu pour le rapporter. (*Pause*).

Student: Ils pensent qu'il a donné le portefeuille à l'autre individu pour le rapporter.

Teacher: Comment meurt-il. (*Pause*).

Student: Il meurt dans le délire.

Teacher: Il meurt dans le délire. (*Pause*).

Student: Il meurt dans le délire.

6. *True-false exercise. Repeat the following sentences, then add "c'est vrai" or "c'est faux." Then you will hear "c'est vrai" or "c'est faux." Repeat it.*

Teacher: Pour un Normand la chose la plus insignifiante a de la valeur. (*Pause*).

Student: Pour un Normand la chose la plus insignifiante a de la valeur. C'est faux.

Teacher: C'est faux. (*Pause*).

Student: C'est faux.

Teacher: Hauchecorne ne met pas la ficelle dans sa poche. (*Pause*).

Student: Hauchecorne ne met pas la ficelle dans sa poche. C'est faux.

Teacher: C'est faux. (*Pause*).

Student: C'est faux.

Teacher: Il cherche dans la poussière comme s'il avait perdu quelque chose. (*Pause*).

Student: Il cherche dans la poussière comme s'il avait perdu quelque chose. C'est vrai.

Teacher: C'est vrai. (*Pause*).

Student: C'est vrai.

Teacher: Un portefeuille n'a pas été perdu sur la route de Goderville. (*Pause*).

Student: Un portefeuille n'a pas été perdu sur la route de Goderville. C'est faux.

Teacher: C'est faux. (*Pause*).

Student: C'est faux.

Teacher: Au milieu du grand repas à l'auberge un gendarme entre. (*Pause*).

Student: Au milieu du grand repas à l'auberge un gendarme entre. C'est vrai.

Teacher: C'est vrai. (*Pause*).

Student: C'est vrai.

Teacher: Hauchecorne accuse Malandain d'avoir trouvé le portefeuille perdu. (*Pause*).

Student: Hauchecorne accuse Malandain d'avoir trouvé le portefeuille perdu. C'est faux.

Teacher: C'est faux. (*Pause*).

Student: C'est faux.

Teacher: "J'ai ramassé de l'argent" répond Hauchecorne. (*Pause*).

Student: "J'ai ramassé de l'argent" répond Hauchecorne. C'est faux.

Teacher: C'est faux. (*Pause*).

Student: C'est faux.

Teacher: On fouille dans la poche de Malandain et on trouve le portefeuille. (*Pause*).

Student: On fouille dans la poche de Malandain et on trouve le portefeuille. C'est faux.

Teacher: C'est faux. (*Pause*).

Student: C'est faux.

Teacher: Hauchecorne ne raconte l'histoire de la ficelle à personne. (*Pause*).

Student: Hauchecorne ne raconte l'histoire de la ficelle à personne. C'est faux.

Teacher: C'est faux. (*Pause*).

Student: C'est faux.

Teacher: Personne ne se moque de lui. (*Pause*).

Student: Personne ne se moque de lui. C'est faux.

Teacher: C'est faux. (*Pause*).

Student: C'est faux.

7. *Practice in antonyms. Give a word which has the opposite meaning of the word you hear. You will hear the correct answer. Repeat it.*

Teacher: économe (*Pause*).

Student: dépensier

Teacher: dépensier (*Pause*).

Student: dépensier

Teacher: insignifiante (*Pause*).

Student: importante

Teacher: importante (*Pause*).

Student: importante

Teacher: un ennemi (*Pause*).

Student: un ami

Teacher: un ami (*Pause*).

Student: un ami

Teacher: il cherche (*Pause*).

Student: il trouve

Teacher: il trouve (*Pause*).

Student: il trouve

Teacher: il a perdu (*Pause*).

Student: il a trouvé

Teacher: il a trouvé (*Pause*).

Student: il a trouvé

Teacher: là-bas (*Pause*).

Student: ici

Teacher: ici (*Pause*).

Student: ici
Teacher: furieux (*Pause*).
Student: calme
Teacher: calme (*Pause*).
Student: calme
Teacher: tout le monde (*Pause*).
Student: personne
Teacher: personne (*Pause*).
Student: personne
Teacher: la justice (*Pause*).
Student: l'injustice
Teacher: l'injustice (*Pause*).
Student: l'injustice
Teacher: il sourit (*Pause*).
Student: il pleure
Teacher: il pleure (*Pause*).
Student: il pleure

8. *Dictée. 1ere lecture: Ecoutez d'abord:*

Hauchecorne / un paysan normand / très économe / ramasse une ficelle / sur la route. / Son ennemi / Malandain / l'accuse / d'avoir trouvé / un portefeuille. / Un autre individu / rapporte l'objet perdu. / Mais personne / ne croit Hauchecorne, / et il meurt / de cette injustice. /

2e lecture: Maintenant écrivez.
3e lecture: Corrigez votre dictée.

The following illustrative lessons employ a format similar to that of the drills on "La Ficelle" given above. They are presented here in summary form.

ILLUSTRATIVE LESSONS

Auditory Comprehension

(Elementary French)

LA FEMME FRANÇAISE DANS LA VIE MODERNE

(Prepared in the Language Laboratory Project of the Bureau of Audio-Visual Instruction, New York City.)

I. *Here are some words to help you understand the passage which will be read to you. You will hear them once in English, twice in French. Repeat only the French words during each pause.*

le statut (*Pause*)	status (*Pause*)	le statut (*Pause*)
le siècle (*Pause*)	century (*Pause*)	le siècle (*Pause*)
le poste (*Pause*)	position (*Pause*)	le poste (*Pause*)
le chimiste (*Pause*)	chemist (*Pause*)	le chimiste (*Pause*)
l'ingénieur (*Pause*)	engineer (*Pause*)	l'ingénieur (*Pause*)
entre autres (*Pause*)	among others (*Pause*)	entre autres (*Pause*)

II. *Now listen to the passage.*

Le statut de la femme en France a beaucoup changé pendant les dix dernières années. Au début du vingtième siècle peu de femmes en France occupaient des postes importants dans la vie économique. Mais la situation n'est pas la même aujourd'hui. Il y a des femmes dans toutes les professions—entre autres, des journalistes, des chimistes, des médecins, des ingénieurs, des avocats.

III. *(Spaced Reading.) Here is the passage again. Repeat in each pause the phrase you have just heard (Spaced re-reading of the entire passage).*

IV. *Answer the following questions. Each question will be heard twice; you are to answer in the pause that follows. Then you will hear the correct answer, followed by a pause. Repeat the correct answer.*

Question: Le statut de la femme en France a-t-il beaucoup changé? (*Repeat, pause*).

Réponse: Oui. Le statut de la femme en France a beaucoup changé. (*Pause*).

Question: Quand le statut de la femme a-t-il changé? (*Repeat, pause*).

Réponse: Le statut de la femme a changé pendant les dix dernières années. (*Pause*).

Question: Est-ce que beaucoup de femmes occupent des postes importants aujourd'hui? (*Repeat, pause*).

Réponse: Oui. Beaucoup de femmes occupent des postes importants aujourd'hui. (*Pause*).

Question: Y a-t-il maintenant des femmes médecins et des femmes avocats? (*Repeat, pause*).

Réponse: Oui. Il y a maintenant des femmes médecins et des femmes avocats. (*Pause*).

V. *Repeat each of the following statements. Then add "c'est vrai" if it is true, "c'est faux" if it is false. You will hear the correct answer.*

Question: Le statut de la femme en France est toujours le même. (*Pause*).

Réponse: C'est faux.

Question: Au début du vingtième siècle peu de femmes occupaient des postes importants. (*Repeat, pause*).

The Language Laboratory / 1 3 3

Réponse: C'est vrai.

Question: Aujourd'hui il n'y a pas de femmes journalistes. (*Repeat, pause*).

Réponse: C'est faux.

Question: Aujourd'hui il y a des femmes dans toutes les professions. (*Repeat, pause*).

Réponse: C'est vrai.

VI. *Dictée. First reading: listen.*

La femme française moderne / ne passe pas / tout son temps / dans la cuisine. / Elle a maintenant sa place / dans toutes les professions. *Second reading: write.*

Third reading: correct your dictation.

Auditory Comprehension
(French 5)
LE FEU ET LE FOU (1ere partie)

(Prepared in the Language Laboratory Project of the Bureau of Audio-Visual Instruction, New York City.)

I. *Commencons la lecture (jusqu'a la p. 69, l. 23).*

II. *Vocabulaire. Voici quelques expressions et quelques mots employés dans la première partie de cette histoire. Vous les entendrez une fois en anglais, deux fois en français. Répétez seulement les mots français pendant les pauses.*

to take a trip	faire un voyage (*Pause, repeat, pause*).
head cold	un rhume de cerveau (*Pause, repeat, pause*).
throat	la gorge (*Pause, repeat, pause*).
to claim	avoir la prétention (*Pause, repeat, pause*).
mad, crazy	fou (*Pause, repeat, pause*).
such	tel (*Pause, repeat, pause*).
match	une allumette (*Pause, repeat, pause*).
instead of	au lieu de (*Pause, repeat, pause*).
to watch, look after	surveiller (*Pause, repeat, pause*).
to prevent	empêcher (*Pause, repeat, pause*).
to go out	s'éteindre (*Pause, repeat, pause*).
to lock	fermer à clé (*Pause, repeat, pause*).

III. *Exercice de vocabulaire. Écoutez les mots et les phrases qui suivant. Puis, pendant les pauses, écrivez en français le mot ou l'expression.*

1. faire un voyage—Les deux amis font un beau voyage.—faire un voyage. (*Pause*).
2. un rhume de cerveau—Robert a un rhume de cerveau.—un rhume de cerveau. (*Pause*).

3. la gorge—Il a aussi mal a la gorge.—la gorge. (*Pause*).

4. avoir la prétention—Paul a la prétention de savoir parler français.—avoir la prétention. (*Pause*).

5. fou—Robert n'est pas fou du tout.—fou. (*Pause*).

6. tel—Il est ridicule de dire une telle chose.—tel. (*Pause*).

7. une allumette—Il faut des allumettes pour allumer le feu.—une allumette. (*Pause*).

8. au lieu de—Paul dit "fou" au lieu de "feu."—au lieu de. (*Pause*).

9. surveiller—Le garçon surveille le malade.—surveiller. (*Pause*).

10. empêcher—Il l'empêche de sortir.—empêcher. (*Pause*).

11. s'éteindre—"S'éteindre" n'est pas un synonyme de "sortir."—s'éteindre. (*Pause*).

12. fermer à clé—La porte est fermée à clé.—fermer à clé. (*Pause*).

IV. *Spaced Reading. Reportons-nous à la page 68, l. 1 (lire a la l. 9 de la chambre). Répétez ce que vous entendrez pendant les pauses.*

V. *Repondez en français aux questions suivantes pendant la première pause. Chaque question sera répétée. Vous entendrez ensuite une reponse correcte. Répétez-la.*

Question: En quelle saison les deux Americains font-ils un voyage en France? (*Pause, repeat*).

Réponse: Ils font le voyage en hiver. (*Pause*).

Question: Qu'est-ce que Paul veut faire? (*Pause, repeat*).

Réponse: Il veut aller se promener. (*Pause*).

Question: Quelle maladie Robert a-t-il? (*Pause, repeat*).

Réponse: Il a un rhume de cerveau. (*Pause*).

Question: Comment Paul pronounce-t-il le français? (*Pause, repeat*).

Réponse: Il le prononce très mal. (*Pause*).

Question: Qu'est-ce que le garçon pense de Robert? (*Pause, repeat*).

Réponse: Il pense qu'il est fou. (*Pause*).

VI. *Écoutez bien les phrases suivantes. Répétez-les pendant les pauses.*

1. Il allume le feu. (*Pause*).   Il regarde le fou. (*Pause*).

2. Il a faim. (*Pause*).   Cherchez la femme. (*Pause*).

3. Ses chevaux sont fatigués. (*Pause*).   Ses cheveux sont longs. (*Pause*).

4. Le poisson nage. (*Pause*).   Le poison tue. (*Pause*).

5. Mon père est bon. (*Pause*).   Ma mère est bonne. (*Pause*).

6. Ma cousine est riche. (*Pause*).   Ma cuisine est moderne. (*Pause*).

VII. *Répétez chacune des phrases suivantes. Puis ajoutez: "C'est vrai" ou "C'est faux." Vous entendrez ensuite la réponse correcte.*

1. Les deux Americains font un voyage en hiver. (*Pause*).   C'est vrai.

2. Paul parle français comme un Parisien. (*Pause*).   C'est faux.
3. Robert a un rhume de cerveau. (*Pause*). C'est vrai.
4. Paul cherche les mots dans un dictionnaire. (*Pause*).   C'est vrai.
5. Le garçon comprend très bien ce que dit Paul. (*Pause*).   C'est faux.
6. Le garçon a peur de Robert. (*Pause*).   C'est vrai.

Auditory Comprehension

(German Level III: Teacher's Script)

1. *Was tut man bei einer solchen Versammlung?*

Der Wiener Opernball, der in dem weltberühmten Wiener Opernhaus rich jähl stattfindet, ist der glanzvolle Höhepunkt und das internationale Ereignis der europäischen Karnevalsaison. Er findet gewöhnlich Anfang Februar in Wien statt. Zahlreiche berühmte Persönlichkeiten aus Europa und Amerika lassen für das wohlbekannte Wiener Ballfest Logen reservieren, die in kurzer Zeit ausverkauft sind. Wenn es Winterspiele irgendwo in der Nähe gibt, dann nehmen die Besucher auch daran teil; danach besuchen sie Wien, um sich dort zu amüsieren.

2. *Auf welche Weise wurde diesem Herrn das Leben gerettet?*

Ein deutscher Schäferhund musste mit dem Leben dafür büssen, dass er eine Hunde-Heldentat vollbrachte, um seinem Herrn das Leben zu retten. Dieser schilderte den Verlust seines Hundes auf der Polizei folgenderweise: Zwei Banditen in jugendlichem Alter traten in sein Geschäft ein und drängten ihn, den Ladenbesitzer, in ein Hinterzimmer, wo zufälligerweise der Hund lag. Der Hund sprang auf und biss den einen jungen Mann in den Arm; der zweite, aber, der ein Messer in der Hand hatte, fiel hierauf wütend auf den Hund und verwundete ihn tötlich. Sogleich liefen die Banditen davon und liessen den Mann auf dem Boden liegen.

3. *Warum flüchteten diese zwei jungen Arbeiter?*

Zwei jugendliche Lehrlinge aus der Sowjetzone erreichten die deutsche Bundesrepublik nach einer langen Wanderung. Zweiundfünfzig Meilen waren sie von ihrer Heimatstadt bis an die Grenze gewandert. Im Schutz der Dunkelheit konnten sie über die Zonengrenze fliehen, ohne dass sie entdeckt wurden. Als man sie fragte, warum sie das getan hätten, erklärten sie, dass sie dadurch ihre Einziehung in die Zonenarmee verhindern wollten.

4. *Welchen Plan schlägt dieser Herr vor?*

Ein englischer Edelmann hat im britischen Oberhaus eine sonderbare Anfrage eingebracht. Der englische Graf glaubt nämlich, dass die Engländer eine allgemeine Tendenz zu grösserem Körperwachstum beweisen und deshalb längere Betten nötig haben. Was will er mit seiner parlamentarischen Anfrage erreichen? Folgendes:—Es sollen nun viele neue Gebäude gebaut werden von öffentlichen Geldern unterstützt. Der Edelmann verlangt, dass das britische Wohnungsministerium es zur Pflicht machen soll, in den Schlafzimmern der Neubauten soviel Raum zu lassen, dass darin Betten für diese sogenannte grössere Körperlänge aufgestellt werden können.

5. *Warum sollte man sich für dieses Buch interessieren?*

Vicki Baum ist der Name einer wohlbekannten Schriftstellerin, die vor kurzem gestorben ist. Ihre Bücher gehören zu den meistgelesenen und meistübersetzten unserer Zeit. Ihre grosse Lesergemeinde erwarb sie durch gewaltige Handlungen, eine lebhafte Erzählungsweise und einen flüssigen Stil. Kurz vor ihrem Tode hat sie ihr letztes Buch vollendet—der Titel: "Es war alles ganz anders." Ihr Leserkreis ist gross und wird wahrscheinlich durch dieses letzte Buch noch grösser werden. Es wurde meistens für ihre Freunde geschrieben, auch für alle, die Freude haben an einer reizvollen Beschreibung der europäischen Kulturentwicklung der letzten fünfzig Jahre.

(Student's question paper)

1. *Was tut man bei einer solchen Versammlung?*
   a. Man lernt Skilaufen.
   b. Man hört eine wohlbekannte Oper.
   c. Man besucht die Sehenswürdigkeiten der Stadt.
   d. Man zieht sich die schönsten Kleider an und tanzt.

2. *Auf welche Weise wurde diesem Herrn das Leben gerettet?*
   a. Das Tier bellte so laut, dass die Polizei sofort hineinstürzte.
   b. Viele Nachbarn folgten dem Jungen in den Laden.
   c. Das Tier hat seine scharfen Zähne benutzt.
   d. Der Herr verliess den Laden durch das Hinterzimmer.

3. *Warum flüchteten diese zwei jungen Arbeiter?*
   a. Sie haben Freunde in Westdeutschland besuchen wollen.
   b. Es gefiel ihnen nicht, in der Sowjetzone zu dienen.
   c. Sie hatten das Wandern sehr gern.
   d. Sie wollten erfahren, wie weit die Grenze von ihrer Heimat war.

4. *Welchen Plan schlägt dieser Herr vor?*
   a. Die neuen Wohnungen sollen im allgemeinen kleiner sein.
   b. Das britische Oberhaus sollte keine Versammlungen mehr halten.
   c. Es müsste in der Zukunft grössere Schlafzimmer in den neuen Wohnungen geben.
   d. Die Regierung sollte die Armen mit viel Geld unterstützen.
5. *Warum sollte man sich für dieses Buch interessieren?*
   1. Es erzählt von dem deutsch-französischen Krieg.
   2. Es ist ein gewaltiger lebhafter Roman.
   3. Es ist eine kulturelle Schilderung der Vergangenheit.
   4. Es handelt sich um die Freunde der Schriftstellerin.

ILLUSTRATIVE LESSON

Aural Comprehension

(Spanish Level III: Teacher's Script)

1. ¿Qué le gustaría al estudiante? Yo había hablado mucho de la Cortina de Hierro, dijo con pena el señor Gomez, estudiante de las Bellas Artes. —Yo creo que hemos sufrido bastante. Ahora solamente quisieramos estudiar en paz alguna ciudad de Occidente. Nada más que estudiar.

2. ¿Cómo se gana la vida este hombre? Hijo de un banderillero, Paco tenía apenas 18 años cuando tomó la alternativa después de intensa actuación como novillero. Su primer año como matador en España era 1960. Desde entonces Paco ha matado mucho torros, casi siempre en forma brilliante.

3. ¿Dónde se habla del arte moderna? El arte moderna, que en los Estados Unidos ya es una cosa vieja, en Rusia todavía da mucho que hablar y que callar. En las calles de Moscú, en los cafés, en los subterraneos, y en los museos, se polemizaba recientemente sobre este tema.

4. ¿Dónde se ve el Japón moderno? El Japón moderno es un país de gran desarrollo industrial y la verdad es que Vd. no podrá comprenderlo si no ve sus industrias. Vd. tiene que visitar al Japón porque es símbolo del mundo moderno e industrial.

5. ¿Por qué tenían que salir los refugiados? Durante largos meses desde que los terremotos y las erupciones volcánicas los obligaron a salir de su isla, los refugiados en la Gran Bretaña vieron por la primera vez árboles altos, aceras urbanas, el tránsito de vehículos y

las casas grandes. También, los refugiados ensayaron el twist y conocieron la televisión. Pero, votaron por volver a su isla.

6. ¿Quiénes constituyan el poder legislativo y judicial? Atenas era una democracia simple y directa. Solamente los varones de más de 18 años podían participar en las asambleas. Ellos constituyan el poder legislativo y judicial.

7. ¿Como se gana la vida la gente de la isla? La economía de la isla, igual como la alimentación, es la papa. Cada parte de los jardines corresponde a determinadas familias, y la propiedad de cada familia se transmite por herencia. En el pasado, la familia más rica era la familia que tenía más papas en su jardín.

8. ¿Qué medicina necesitan personas tristes? Los tranquilizadores alivían a la gente tensa y nerviosa que debe ser apaciguada. Pero los tranquilizadores pueden hacer daño a un número mayor de personas que se sienten tristes, sin energía, crónicamente decaídas. Esta gente triste necesita energizantes, no tranquilizadores.

9. ¿Dónde trabajaba el hombre? En el fondo del bosque, entre un grupo de árboles, vivía un pobre hombre que se llamaba Narces. Era bajo, amarillo y triste. En su juventud había sido actor de teatro de aldea. Llevaba barba y monóculo, y no peinaba nunca, como se había acostumbrado en las comedias del teatro.

10. ¿Cómo era la cultura cuando los españoles vinieron? La extensa región que comprende el Yucatán, Guatemala y Honduras, poseo la cultura tal vez más alta de la época precolombiana. Era la cultura maya. Cuando los españoles llegaron, las grandes ciudades habían desaparecido, y muchos importantes monumentos estaban sumergidos en la densa vegetación del trópico.

(Student's question paper)

1. *¿Qué le gustaría al estudiante?*
   a. le gustaría jugar
   b. le gustaría estudiar
   c. le gustaría sufrir
   d. le gustaría viajar
2. *¿Cómo se gana la vida este hombre?*
   a. como actor
   b. como doctor
   c. como alternativo
   d. como matador
3. *¿Dónde se habla del arte moderna?*
   a. en todas partes de Rusia
   b. en todas partes de los Estados Unidos

c. en las cuevas

d. en los museos

4. *¿Dónde se ve el Japón moderno?*
   a. en el campo
   b. en las ciudades industriales
   c. en los símbolos
   d. en lo moderno

5. *¿Por qué tenían que salir los refugiados?*
   a. porque no había paz
   b. porque había tempestades
   c. porque no había caminos
   d. porque votaron volver a su isla

6. *¿Quiénes constituyan el poder legislativo y judicial?*
   a. las mujeres
   b. los niños
   c. los hombres
   d. toda la gente

7. *¿Cómo se gana la vida la gente de la isla?*
   a. como agricultores
   b. como médicos
   c. como marineros
   d. como pastores

8. *¿Qué medicina necesitan personas tristes?*
   a. energizantes
   b. tranquilizadores
   c. recetas
   d. no necesitan medicinas

9. *¿Dónde trabajaba el hombre?*
   a. en el bosque
   b. con pobres
   c. en el teatro
   d. no trabajaba

10. *¿Cómo era la cultura cuando los españoles vinieron?*
    a. era pobre
    b. casi había desaparecido
    c. había monumentos
    d. era rica

Appendix

BIBLIOGRAPHY OF LANGUAGE LABORATORIES AND TECHNIQUES

Ahles, Richard F., "French Needn't Be Greek Any More," *University Alumnus*, May, 1959.

Archer, John B., *The Philosophy of the Language Laboratory*. Reports of the Working Committees, 1957 Northeast Conference on the Teaching of Foreign Languages. Nelson Brooks, MAT Program. New Haven, Conn.: Yale University.

Barrow, Mrs. Richard, "The New Way to Teach Foreign Languages," *School Management*, November, 1958.

Borglum, Geo. P., "Revolution in the Teaching of Modern Foreign Languages," *School and Society*, Vol. 79 (1954), pp. 129–34.

Borglum, G., and Mueller, T., "Audio-Visual Language Teaching," *French Review*, May, 1958.

Brooks, Nelson, *Report of Committee on Tests*. Committee Reports, 1954. NEA Conference.

Council of Chief State School Officers, *Purchase Guide for Programs in Science, Mathematics, and Modern Foreign Languages*. Ginn & Co. 1959.

———, *Standards for Materials and Equipment for the Improvement of Instruction in Science, Mathematics, and Foreign Languages*. Washington, D.C.: Council of Chief State School Officers.

de Mandach, André B., *A Bibliography of Audio-Visual Aids and Techniques in Language Teaching*. $1.00.

———, *Supplement to a Bibliography of Audio-Visual Aids and Techniques in Language Teaching.* Shakespeare Tape Library, 1818 M St., N.W., Washington, D.C. 25 cents.

de Mandach, André B., and Bates, Jefferson D. *Setting up your own little language lab: a low-cost recipe.* Shakespeare Tape Library, 1818 M St., N.W., Washington, D.C., 1954.

Dostert, L. E., "The Georgetown Institute Language Program," Publications of the Modern Language Association, April, 1953, pp. 3–12.

Eddy, Frederick D., *The Secondary School Language Laboratory: Some Observations on Present Practice and Long Range Possibilities.* Reports of the 1956 Northeast Conference on the Teaching of Foreign Languages. Nelson Brooks, MAT Program. New Haven, Conn.: Yale University.

Eddy, Frederick D., and Hocking, Elton. "Language Learning Today," *Audio-Visual Instruction,* September, 1959.

Educational Screen. Audio-visual magazine. 64 E. Lake St., Chicago, Ill.

Etmekjian, James. *Pattern Drills in Language Teaching.* New York: New York University Press, 1966.

Finn, James D., *The Audio-Visual Equipment Manual.* New York: Dryden Press, 1957.

Fulton, Renée, "Language Laboratory Develops the Listening Ear," *Modern Language Journal,* May, 1959.

Gaarder, A. Bruce, *Foreign Language Laboratory Techniques.* Supplement of News-Letter of Louisiana Foreign Language Teachers Association. Baton Rouge, 1956.

Gaudin, Lois, "The Language Laboratory," *French Review,* February, 1952.

Harris, Cleland C., *The Use of Mechanical Aids in the Language Program at L.S.U., Hispania,* 1949, pp. 20–26.

Havighurst, Robert J., "Aids to Language Study," *School and Society,* 1949, p. 444.

Hayes, Alfred S., *Technical Guide for the Selection, Purchase, Use and Maintenance of Language Laboratory Facilities.* U.S. Office of Education, Bulletin 1963, No. 37, 1963.

Heath, Douglas L., *A Language Laboratory Handbook and Directory for 1956.* How to Plan, Build, and Operate a Modern Language Laboratory. Language Training Aids. Boyds, Maryland.

Hirsch, Ruth, *Audio-Visual Aids in Language Teaching.* Monograph No. 5. Institute of Languages and Linguistics. Washington, D.C.: Georgetown University, 1954.

Hocking, Elton, "The Purdue Language Program." *PMLA,* September, 1955. Part II. Publications of the Modern Language Association of America. New York 3, N.Y.

Hocking, Elton, and Merchant, Robert C., "The Fabulous Language Labs," *Educational Screen and Audio-Visual Guide,* April, 1959.

"How Five Schools Use Foreign Language Labs," *School Management,* June, 1959.

Huebener, Theodore, "Audio-Visual Aids in High School," *Modern Language Journal,* October, 1959.

Johnston, Marjorie C., *Modern Foreign Languages in the High Schools.* Bulletin 1958, No. 16. $1.00. Washington, D.C.: U.S. Dept. of Health, Education, and Welfare, Office of Education.

Johnston, Marjorie C., and Seerley, Catherine C., *Foreign Language Laboratories in Schools and Colleges.* 1959 Bulletin No. 3. Washington, D.C.: U.S. Dept. of Health, Education, and Welfare, Office of Education.

————, "The Foreign Language Laboratory," *School Life,* December, 1958.

King, P. E., "Continuing Study on Modern Language Laboratories." New York: Magnetic Recording Industries, 1958.

Kone, Elliott H., *Language Laboratories: Modern Techniques in Teaching Foreign Languages.* Annual Bulletin 19. Connecticut Audio-Visual Education Association. $2.00. Educational Film Library Association, 250 West 57th St., New York 19, or Yale University Audio-Visual Center, New Haven, Conn.

Lloyd, Donald J., "Language in a Living Environment," *Audio-Visual Instruction,* February, 1958.

Locke, William N., *Advice for the Lab-lorn.* Bay State Foreign Language Bulletin, October, 1958. Amherst, Mass.: University of Massachusetts.

————, "Ideal Language Laboratory Equipment," *Modern Language Journal,* January, 1959.

Marty, Fernand L., "Language Laboratory Techniques," *Educational Screen,* February, 1956.

————, *Methods and Equipment for the Language Laboratory.* Middlebury, Vt.: Audio-Visual Publications, 1956.

Mazzara, Richard A., "Now that we have a language laboratory, what do we do with it?" *French Review,* May, 1959.

McGraw, Myrtle B., "The Role of the Teacher and Student in the Electronic World," *Modern Language Journal,* May, 1959.

Modern Language Association. Foreign Language Program. *Materials List.* September, 1959. MLA, 4 Washington Pl., New York 3, N.Y.

——, *Materials for Use by Teachers of Modern Foreign Languages.* Ed. by Douglas W. Alden. George Banta Co., Menasah, Wis., 1959.

——, *The Language Laboratory.* Foreign Language Bulletin No. 39. MLA, 4 Washington Pl., New York 3, N.Y.

Modern Language Journal, May, 1959. Issue devoted to language laboratory.

Young, Biloine, "A Do-It Yourself Language Laboratory."

Fulton, Renée J., "Language Laboratories Develop the Listening Ear."

McGraw, Myrtle B., "The Role of the Teacher and Student in the Electronic World."

Sanchez, José, "Twenty Years of Language Laboratory." Annotated Bibliography.

Siciliano, E., "An Experiment in Listening Comprehension."

Najam, Edward. (Ed.). *Materials and Techniques for the Language Laboratory.* Report of the Language Laboratory Conference Held at Purdue University, Mar. 23–25, 1961. Bloomington, Ind.: Publication 18 of the Indiana University Research Center in Anthropology, Folklore and Linguistics, 1962.

Newmark, Maxim, *Twentieth Century Modern Language Teaching.* New York: Philosophical Library, 1947.

O'Neil, James, "Men, Machines, and Conversation Courses," *French Review,* May, 1953.

Pleasants, Jeanne Varney, *Language Laboratory Techniques.* Reports of the Working Committees, 1957 Northeast Conference on the Teaching of Foreign Languages. Nelson Brooks, MAT Program, Yale University, New Haven, Conn.

——, *Teaching Aids and Techniques.* Reports of the Working Committees, 1955 Northeast Conference on the Teaching of Foreign Languages. Germaine Bree, N.Y.U., editor. Nelson Brooks, MAT Program, Yale University, New Haven, Conn.

"Purdue University's Electronic Language Laboratory," *Audio-Visual Guide,* February, 1953.

Rossellt, La Velle, "Audio-Visual Techniques in Foreign Language Teaching," *Modern Language Journal,* 1949, pp. 544–50.

The Secondary School Language Laboratory: Some Observations on Present Practices and Long Range Possibilities. Report of the Working Committees of the 1956 Northeast Conference on the Teaching of Foreign Languages. Nelson Brooks, MAT Program, Yale University, New Haven, Conn.

Stack, Edward M., *The Language Laboratory and Modern Language Teaching.* Fair Lawn, N.J.: Oxford University Press, 1960.

Switzer, Rebecca, "A-V Aids in Teaching Modern Foreign Languages," *Hispania,* 1948, pp. 68–69.

Ruark, Henry C., Jr., (ed.). *The Audio-Visual Equipment Directory. A Guide to Current Models of Audio-Visual Equipment.* National Audio-Visual Association, Fairfax, Va., 1958.

Using Laboratory Techniques in Teaching Foreign Languages in New York City Schools. NYBE Curriculum Research Report, 1961. Paper. $0.50. 60 pp.

Van Eenenaam, Evelyn, "Annotated Bibliography of Modern Language Methodology for 1956," *Modern Language Journal,* January, 1958.

Whitehouse, Robert S., "The Workshop: A Language Laboratory," *Hispania,* 1945, pp. 88–90.

"What Do We Know About Modern Language Teaching?" Symposium, *Audio-Visual Instruction,* September, 1959.

Wojnowski, Margaret, *Emphasis on Understanding and Speaking: The Foreign Language Laboratory.* Bulletin, 1958, No. 16: "Modern Foreign Languages in High School." Washington, D.C.: U.S. Dept. of Health, Education, and Welfare, Office of Education.

French

TEACHERS' GUIDES

Cadoux, Remunda. *French for Secondary Schools. N. Y. State,* 1960. 205 pp. Free in N.Y. State; $1.00 out of state.

A carefully planned and well organized syllabus for secondary schools. Detailed instructions are given for the use of pattern drills and audio-lingual procedures.

Modern Language Association. *MLA Teacher's Guide: French in Grade Four.* Educational Publishing Corp., Darien, Conn., 1956. $2.50.

Colman, Charles W., Carter, Boyd G., and Nordon, Denise. *French for Children—A Manual for Teachers and Parents.* Lincoln, Neb.: Johnson Publishing Co., 1955. $1.25.

Modern Language Association. *MLA Teacher's Guide: Beginning French in Grade Three.* Darien, Conn: Educational Publishing Corp., 1959. $2.50.

Dunkel, Harold B., and Roger A. Pillet. *French in the Elementary School: Five Years' Experience.* Chicago, 1962. 150 pp. $3.75.

An evaluation of a five-year experiment (1955–60) in the University of Chicago Elementary School. The various problems in connection with FLES are taken up and solutions offered.

Foreign Language Revision Program for Secondary Schools. French. Levels I and II. Curriculum Bulletin 2a. 1962–63 Series. New York City Board of Education. 1962. 79 pp. Paper. $1.00.

———, Level III. NYBE Curriculum Bulletin 1963–64 series. 71 pp. Paper. $1.00.

———, Level IV. NYBE Curriculum Bulletin 1964–65 series. 39 pp. Paper. $1.00.

Produced by an impressive committee of teachers and language experts under the chairmanship of Theodore Huebener. These bulletins are well-organized and describe the latest materials and procedures in detail.

French for Elementary Schools. Albany: University of the State of N.Y., 1966. 44 pp. Paper. Free in N.Y. State.

An excellent outline of an elementary school program in French.

COURSES

French for Elementary Schools. Consultant Vera Villegas. Filmed in U.S. McGraw-Hill, 1960. 2 sets of 6 filmstrips. 50–60 frames each. Captions in French. Color. Three 10 in. $33\frac{1}{3}$ rpm. discs with scripts. $57.50, with discs and Teacher's Guide.

Attractive filmstrips. Pictures shown first without and then with captions. Stress, however, is on American customs.

French for Children. Frederick D. Eddy (ed.). Native speakers. Ottenheimer, 1957. Two 10 in. $33\frac{1}{3}$ rpm. discs. $4.95 each.

Everyday situations presented in familiar form. Very pleasing children's voices.

French Auditory Comprehension Exercises, Level II, Units 1 & 2.
Educational Audio Visual, 1963. Two 5 in. 3¾ ips. single-track
tapes; teacher's guide with full text, 1 pad of student work sheets
containing questions. $11.90. Additional student pads of 100
sheets at $1.50.

Good for classroom and laboratory. There are 15 paragraphs and
questions for listening comprehension. Pauses of one minute allow
for student to give correct answer.

Circling the Globe with Speech: French I, II & III. Wilmac, 1954,
1956 and 1959. Three 12 in. 33⅓ rpm. discs. $5.95 each. Text.

Very good for teaching pronunciation, intonation, and culture.
Students from various parts of France describe their home towns
and their daily activities.

Circling the Globe with Speech: French—Simplified, Vols. I & II.
Wilmac, 1961. Two 12 in. 33⅓ rpm. discs. $5.95 each. Text.

Everyday language used. Good for pronunciation and intonation.
Life in various parts of France is described.

Regents Auditory and Reading Comprehension Exercises in French.
Recorded by Thompson Ramo Wooldridge. Regents, 1964. One
5 in. 3¾ ips. dual-track plastic tape. $10.50. Student's Text $0.85.
Teacher's Text $1.95.

Excellent for teaching auditory comprehension.

"Parlez-Vous Français?" Heath. Six 6 in. discs. $7.53.

Selections from the "Introductory Lessons" and reading passages
of the first-year textbook, "Parlez-Vous Français?" by Huebener
and Neuschatz (2nd ed.).

Circling the Globe with Speech: French. Wilmac. One 12 in. disc.
$5.67.

Seven French students speak of life in their homes.

Pei, Mario. *Getting Along in French, Vol. I.* Folkways, 1962. One
12 in. 33⅓ rpm. disc. $5.95. Text.

Situations encountered by a tourist in France. Supplementary.

Pathescope-Berlitz Audio-Visual French Language Series. Pathescope, 1959. Eight sets of 5 lessons each to be used as supplement
to basic course. Graded for a 2 or 3 year sequence. Each set: 5 filmstrips. 35 mm. Color. Average 45 frames each. Filmed in France.
Dialogues by native speakers. Each set: three 10 in. 33⅓ rpm.
discs or three 5 in. 3¾ ips. plastic two-track tape reels. Teacher's
guide and scripts. $81.12 a set (five lessons). Four sets $281.28.
Eight sets $537.12. Extra scripts 100 for $3.00. *Listening Compre-*

hension Tests. Pathescope, 1961. One for each lesson and 4 review tests. Recorded by native speakers. Two 7 in. 3¾ ips. plastic two-track tape reels. About 1½ hours each. $18.75 a reel. Printed tests and answer key. Extra tests 100 for $3.00.

An interesting and colorful presentation of French life.

A-LM French: Level One. Mary P. Thompson, Sharon Entwhistle, Marilyn Ray. Harcourt, 1961. Student Text (15 booklets including index). About 180 pp. $1.86. Teaching Tests $0.36. Student Binder $1.50. Practice Record Set, fourteen 7 in. 33⅓ rpm. discs. $5.55. Classroom/Laboratory Record Set, fifteen 12 in. 33⅓ rpm. discs. $30.00. Classroom/Laboratory Tape Set, thirty-six 5 in. 3¾ ips. reels $75.00, or eighteen 7 in. 7½ ips. reels $60.00. (Classroom/Laboratory discs and tapes have identical contents.) Teacher's Manual and Teacher's Desk Materials (Student Binder, one set of Student Text booklets, control sheets, Audio Index, and Teaching Tests) free to purchasers.

Good program for developing audio-lingual facility. Good voices, units well-planned, although procedures may become boring after a while.

Parlons Français. Modern Language Project of the Massachusetts Council for Public Schools. Ch. Wm. M. Locke, Dirs. Gordon R. Silber and Earle S. Randall. Head teacher Anne Slack. Heath-De-Roch, 1961. 60 films av. 15 min. each. 16 or 8 mm. Filmed in U.S. and France. Eight teacher preparation films. Each film: color $137.50 (16 mm.), $95.00 (8 mm.); b & w $90.00 (16 mm.), $70.00 (8 mm.). Forty 7 in. 33⅓ rpm. discs (in 8 albums) for pupils. Each album (5 discs) $2.00. Set of 8 albums $12.50. Teacher preparation discs also. Teacher's guides with verbatim script. Pupil activity books. Full course: color, 16 mm. $75.00; 8 mm. $55.00; b & w 16 mm. $55.00; 8 mm. $45.00.

Excellent series of films. English is used sparingly.

FILMS AND FILMSTRIPS

La Famille travaille ensemble. Consultant Wilhelmina Hill. Filmed in U.S. Coronet, 1961. 16 mm. 11 min. B & w Purchase $60.00. Script.

A surprise party is being prepared for the father by the mother and two children. Voice and intonation good, but narration rapid.

La Famille française Brunel. Filmed in France. McGraw-Hill, n.d. 16 mm. 17 min. B & w $97.50.

Daily life of a family in Blois. Authentic and interesting.

Vacances en Normandie. Encyclopaedia Britannica Films. French. 11 min. $50.00. Color $100.00.
Latour family takes a trip into Normandy, visits a small village and joins in the festivities. Language used is simple.

Une Famille Bretonne. Encyclopaedia Britannica Films. French. 11 min. $45.00.
Narration in present tense tells story of French children.

French Children. Encyclopaedia Britannica Films. French. 11 min. $50.00.
A Breton family is visited on its farm; daily life and customs are depicted.

France and Its People. Encyclopaedia Britannica Films. 14 min. $75.00. Color $150.00.
The activities of a French family are depicted.

La Famille Martin (Series). International Film Bureau. French. 18 min. $87.50.
A humorous incident in the return of daughter Madeleine from a vacation in England.

Histoire de Poissons. International Film Bureau. French. 13 min. $55.00.
The Martin family procures fish in preparation for a dinner to which the curé has been invited.

Depart de Grandes Vacances. International Film Bureau. French. 11 min. $55.00.
The Martin family is preparing to leave by car for the country. Humorous.

La Vie dans une ferme française. Filmed in France. Coronet. 16 mm. 11 min. Color. Purchase $120.00. B & w $60.00. English captions.
Description of life on a French farm narrated in French.

French Canadians. United World Films. English and French. 11 min. $100.00.
Depicts farmers raising produce and selling it in city markets.

SONGS

French Children's Songs for Teaching French. Folkways FO 8003. Two 10 in. LP discs with text $8.50. Tapes from phono-tapes. 3¾ ips. $5.95 or 7.5 ips. $9.00.

Rondes et Chansons de France. Livres-Disques Philips, Paris. Six records. AATF National Information Bureau, Brooklyn College, N.Y. or Goldsmith's Music Shop, N.Y. 10.

Chansons de France: Parts I, II, III and IV. Familiar French songs and guide with complete text. Color. Each set $6.00. United World Films.

Best-Loved French Folk Songs. Monitor, 1963. One 12 in. 33⅓ rpm. disc. $4.98. Complete text of all songs.
A selection of 24 folk songs, clearly sung, with orchestral accompaniment.

Chants pour les enfants. Songs from "Petites Conversations" and "Mes Premieres Leçons de Français"). Heath. One 12 in. 33⅓ rpm. disc. $3.76.
Contains most of the best-known French children's songs.

Rondes et chansons de France. Performed by Lucienne Vernay and others. Instrumental accompaniment. Disques Philips. Distr. Goldsmith. Ten 7 in. 45 rpm. discs $2.95 each. Text.
Clear diction, normal tempo. Colorful booklet with text and music.

Chansons pour la classe de français. Bowmar Records 1959. Sung by Micheline Bardin, accompanied by an accordion. Recorded in U.S. One 12 in. 33⅓ rpm. disc $4.95. Book of 16 folksongs by Ruth De Cesare. 20 pp. Paper $1.00.
Songs clearly sung. Analysis of vocabulary and unusual expressions is given.

French-Canadian Folk Songs. Folkways. One 10 in. disc. $2.59.
Folk songs reflecting various aspects of French-Canadian life.

French Children's Songs. Folkways. Two 10 in. discs. $5.19.
A collection of well-known French folk songs.

Belles Chansons de France. Casterman, 1956. Illus. 19 pp. $1.50.
A good selection. The pictures are attractive.

Favorite French Folk Songs. Alan Mills. Oak, 1963. Illus. 93 pp. $2.45.
A wide selection of songs with guitar accompaniment. The English translations are good.

LITERATURE

Fables de la Fontaine: Part I. United World Films. $6.00. Text of four fables with illustrations. (1) La Grenouille qui veut se faire aussi grosse que le Boeuf. (2) Le Renard et la Cigogne. (3) Le Lion et le Rat. (4) La Laitière et le Pot au Lait.

Fables de la Fontaine: Part II. United World Films. $6.00. Text with illustrations. (1) Les Voleurs et l'Ane. (2) Le Renard et les Raisins. (3) La Colombe et la Fourmi. (4) Le Corbeau et le Renard. (5) La Cigale et la Fourmi. (6) Le Lièvre et les Grenouilles.

Jean Cocteau Reading in French. Caedmon, 1962. One 12 in. 33⅓ rpm. disc. $5.95.
Excellent reading. No text, however.

Les Pages de Ronsard qu'il faut connaître. L'Encyclopédie Sonore, 1962. Hachette. One 7 in. 33⅓ rpm. disc. $3.50.
Beautiful reading. Suitable for literature course. No text.

An Anthology of French Poetry. Albert Sonnenfeld, (ed.). Performed by Michel Guilloton. Caedmon, 1963. One 12 in. 33⅓ rpm. disc. $5.95. Text.
A selection of 36 poems beautifully read. Some poems suitable for secondary level, some only for advanced students.

Golden Treasury of French Verse. Spoken Arts. One 12 in. disc. $3.63. Text with English translation.
Collection of 28 well-known poems from 15th century to date.

MAPS

France, Physical. Distr. Denoyer. Colored to show land elevations. Boundaries of natural regions indicated. 50 x 40 in. Paper, muslin hand mounted. Palin wood rods $9.50. Spring roller, steel board $15.00. Spring roller, steel case $17.75.

France, Physical. Hatier. Distr. Denoyer. Text in French. Colored. Various basins and plateaus defined and identified by color and names. 40 x 48 in. Plain wood rods $9.50. Spring roller, steel board $13.50. Spring roller, steel case $16.00.

France, Political and Historical. Denoyer. Text in French. Colored. Provinces of 1789. Departments shown by dotted lines. 50 x 40 in. Plain wood rods $9.50. Spring roller, steel board $15.00. Spring roller, steel case $17.75.
Excellent map. Clear colors and labeling. Durable.

Paris, City Plan. Hatier. Distr. Denoyer. Text in French. Important buildings, highways, railroads, etc. 48 x 40 in. Muslin mounted, plain wood rollers $9.50. Spring roller, steel board $13.50. Spring roller, steel case $16.00.

German

German Club Manual. Birkmaier, Emma Marie. Thrift, 1949.
Offers a rich variety of suggestions for stimulating interest
through the language club.

Successful Devices in Teaching German. Wagner, Rudolph E.
Walch, 1959.
Useful ideas for the teacher to secure fluency and accuracy. Also
compares the various dialects of Germany.

Foreign Language Revision Program for Secondary Schools. German. Levels I and II. New York City Board of Education Curriculum Bulletin. September 1962. 63 pp. Paper. $1.00.

────── Level III. 1963–64 Series. No. 2c. 69 pp. Paper. $1.00.
Produced by an impressive committee of teachers and language
experts under the chairmanship of Theodore Huebener. These
bulletins are well-organized and describe the latest materials and
procedures.

RESOURCE LISTS

AATG Selective List of Materials for German FLES. Prepared and
edited by the AATG FLES Committee. Compiled by Mrs. Merriam Moore. Write: Dr. Gerrit Memming, Albrecht College,
Reading, Pa. 19604.

FILMSTRIPS AND SLIDES

Hamburg, die Hansestadt. Filmed in Germany. International Film
Bureau, 1958. 16 mm. 10 min. Narrated in German. Color. Purchase $150.00. Rental $7.50. Student Handbook $0.39. One 7½
ips. tape $7.50.
A good introduction to the business and shopping districts of
Hamburg. Also presents life in a middle-class home.

Heidelberg. Narrators Ruth Pressell and Armin Frank. Filmed in
Germany. International Film Bureau, 1961. 16 mm. 14 min. Narrated in German. Color. Purchase $150.00. Student workbook
$0.39. One 7½ ips. tape reel. 24 min. $7.50.
Excellent views of Heidelberg. Music and festival scenes. Costumes and dances.

Oberbayern. Text by Menno Spann. Filmed in Germany. International Film Bureau, 1960. 16 mm. 15 min. Narrated in German. Color. Purchase $150.00. Student workbook $0.39. One 7½ ips. tape reel, 32 min. $7.50.

Interesting cultural film. Narrator speaks clearly and at normal speed.

Romantische Städt. Filmed in Germany. International Film Bureau, 1961. 16 mm. 13 min. Narrated. Color Purchase $135.00. Rental $7.50. Student Handbook $0.39. One 7½ ips. tape $7.50.

Brief descriptions of what a tourist would see in Munich, Dinkelsbühl and Rothenburg. German enunciation is overly careful.

Der Schwarzwald. Filmed in Germany. International Film Bureau, 1961. 16 mm. 12 min. Narrated. Color purchase $135.00. Rental $6.00. Student Handbook $0.39. One 7½ ips. tape $7.50.

Farms, towns and restors of the Black Forest are shown. The accompanying handbook provides the complete text of the soundtrack. The narration is somewhat slow at times.

Western Germany: The Land and Its People. Coronet Instructional Films. Narrated in English. 11 min. $55.00. Color $110.00.

Portrays the industrial, agricultural and commercial life of West Germany.

German Farm Town. Filmed in Germany. Kleinberg, 1960. 16 mm. 12 min. Sound track with either German or English narration. Available in three different German language versions. Color. Purchase $120.00. Separate tapes of any German track on request $15.00 each.

Many different aspects of farm life, live stock raising and marketing are depicted. Track and tape are done very carefully; recommended for high school students.

Elementary German for Young Americans. Written by José Sanchez and Emmy M. Schreiner. SVE, 1961. 6 filmstrips. Average 48 frames each. Color. Three 12 in. 33⅓ rpm. discs $35.10. English-German Guide.

Excellent for an elementary school program or even a 7th grade class. The vocabulary is of high frequency. New words are repeated twice with spaced pauses for the students to repeat. There is a short easy song at the end of each lesson. Enunciation is clear.

Slides for German. Morthole, 1960. Filmed in Germany, Switzerland and Austria. 35 mm. 19 sets. Average set over 60 slides. Glass mounting. English lecture included in each set of slides. Rental $3.00 plus postage. All slide sets have a tape lecture in English. 6 slide sets also have a tape lecture in German. Each lecture is one 7 in. 3¾ ips. dual track 32 min. plastic tape. Rental $2.00. These slides are of outstanding artistic and technical quality. They can be used effectively at any age level.

Das deutsche Dorf. Written by Glenn Waas. Performed by Lotte Kobler and David Berger. AATG n.d. Filmed in Germany. 35 mm. 24 frames. Color. Three tapes: elementary: one 5 in. 7½ ips. full-track 12 min. plastic tape reel; intermediate: one 5 in. 7½ ips. full-track 16 min. tape reel; advanced: one 5 in. 7½ ips. full-track 16 min. tape reel. Free to AATG members.

This filmstrip with tapes for three levels is an excellent supplement for cultural instruction. The German is clear and well-spoken; the vocabulary is well-chosen. The pictures include home, school, farm scenes.

TAPES AND RECORDINGS

Self-Teaching Record Course: German. Berlitz. Ten 12 in. discs. $75.00.

Living Language: German. Crown. One 10 in. disc. $6.07.

Descriptions and conversations involving proper names, days of the week, months, numbers and adjectives.

Living Language Course: German. Read by authors: Genevieve A. Martin and Theodor Bertram. Crown, 1956. Four 10 in. 33⅓ rpm. discs $9.95. Manual and dictionary. Paper. Extra copies $1.50 each.

The course consists of 40 lessons involving the natural method. The emphasis is upon sentence response. Sentences are not repeated after the response. There are errors in the manual.

Linguaphone. Native speakers from Rundfunk Köln. Linguaphone, 1959. Sixteen 7 in. 45 rpm. or 10 in. 78 rpm. discs $57.00. Thirty-two 5 in. 3¾ ips. single-track plastic tape reels $240.00. Set of 3 Manuals $5.00. Student Workbook $1.00. German Reference Grammar $1.50. Workbook, Part II and Structural Exercises.

The tapes allow time for repetition, the records do not. Material can be used by advanced students to improve speaking ability and to increase vocabulary.

Pathescope-Berlitz Audio-Visual German Series. Pathescope, 1963. Thirty filmstrips, 35 mm., 45 frames, photographs in color.

Eighteen coordinated 5 in. 3¾ ips. dual-track tapes. Approx. 15 min. per tape. Each set has: 5 color filmstrips, 3 tapes, Teacher's Guide, Teacher's English Script, 20 Student's German Scripts. One set (5 lessons) $81.25, three sets (15 lessons) $210.00, six sets (30 lessons) $399.00.

Designed as a full course, these sets can be used effectively for linguistic as well as cultural enrichment. Each set includes "mim-mem" aural drill. Professional quality pictures of authentic scenes in a variety of realistic situations.

A-LM German: Level One. Harcourt, 1961. Student Text (15 booklets) $1.86. Teaching Tests, $0.36. Student Binder $1.50. Practice record set, fourteen 7 in. 33⅓ rpm. discs $5.55. Classroom/Laboratory Set: thirty-six 5 in. 3¾ ips. reels $75.00, or eighteen 7 in. 7½ ips. reels $60.00. (Discs and tapes have identical contents) Teacher's Manual and Teacher's Desk Materials (Student Binder, one set of Student Text booklets, control sheets, audio index, and Teaching Tests) free to purchasers.

The recordings are clear and well-enunciated. The lessons are based on proper grammar sequence, easily introduced by conversations and learned through the drills which accompany each unit.

A-LM German: Level Two. Harcourt, 1964. Nine units plus last 3 units of Level One. $3.80. Practice Record Set (box of nine 7 in. 33⅓ discs) $4.60. Student Test Answer Forms (booklet of 48 perforated pages) $0.60. Classroom/Laboratory Materials: 7½ ips. Tape Set (forty 7 in. full-track, Tenzar reels) $120.00, or 33⅓ rpm. Record Set (twenty-two 12 in. discs) $44.00. 7½ ips. Listening-Comprehension Testing Tape Set (four 7 in. full-track Tenzar reels) $20.00. Teacher's Manual free.

The second level introduces a rather heavy vocabulary load for the learner. The transition between Level I and Level II is abrupt and taxing. The text places an increasing stress on reading and writing while maintaining audio-lingual skills. Narrative is interesting. Many structure drills of various kinds are provided. At times speakers forget they are not speaking to native Germans; endings are dropped and utterances are unclear.

Circling the Globe with Speech. 4 vols. Wilmac, 1954. 3. Darmstadt, Garmisch-Partenkirchen, Berlin, Mannheim, Freiburg, Vienna. II. Flensburg, Hamburg, Lübeck, Reutlingen, Breslau, Offenbach am Main. III. Hamburg, Munich, Isar River and other places.

Each vol. one 12 in. 33⅓ rpm. disc, text $5.95, or one 7 in. 7½ ips. dual-track tape reel, text $8.95.

Excellent discs with different personalities telling about their activities and diversions. Voices are clear and well paced. The diction is good and the speakers are varied.

Von Morgens Früh bis Abends Spät. Parts I and II (Das Deutsche Leben Series). EMC, 1956. One 5 in. 3¾ ips. dual-track 30 min. plastic tape reel $5.95. Script and teacher's guide.

The activities of a German family are reflected through conversations between father, mother, children, their friends and a housekeeper. The doctor talks with patients in his office. The vocabulary is practical and everyday.

German for Children. Frederick D. Eddy, (ed.). Ottenheimer, 1960. Two 10 in. 33⅓ rpm. discs $4.95. Manual for teachers and parents contains script, translation and phrase index. Extra manuals $1.00.

Excellent for elementary school. Voices and topics are for young children. Natural dialogues spoken by native speakers. Pauses for repetition and summary narrations.

Invitation to German Poetry. Compiled by Guy Stern and Gustave Mathieu. Read by Lotte Lenya. Dover, 1959. One 12 in. 33⅓ rpm. disc. 50 min. $4.95 with text. Additional texts $2.50.

Poetry from Walther von der Vogelweide to Bertolt Brecht. Excellent clarity of voice with emotion expressed by intensity. Useful for advanced high school students. Text contains 165 pages and includes full German texts of the poems; also a faithful English translation of each and a portrait, biographical and critical discussion of each poet.

German Lyric Poems. Performed by Lotte Lehmann. Caedmon, 1957. One 12 in. 33⅓ rpm. disc. 60 min. $5.95 with text.

An excellent recording of poems by Goethe, Mörike, Heine, Rilke, Hofmansthal, Müller. Accompanying German text with English translations.

The Golden Treasury of German Verse. Read by Henry Schnitzler. Recorded in U.S. Spoken Arts, 1956. One 12 in. 33⅓ rpm. disc. Texts with translation.

A good selection of German lyrics from the Middle High German period to Bertolt Brecht. Good for advanced course in German literature. Accompanying booklet by Frank G. Ryder and translations by Sam Morgenstern are excellent.

Goethe. Faust: Der Tragödie erster Teil. Performed by Gustaf Gründgens, Paul Hartmann and cast of the Düsseldorfer Schauspielhaus. Deutsche Grammaphon Gesellschaft. Distr. Goldsmith, Lorraine, Rosenberg. Three 12 in. 33⅓ rpm. discs $20.85. Text. Outstanding. Suitable for advanced students.

MAPS AND CHARTS

Deutschland. Harms, 1961. Distr. Denoyer. Text in German. Colored. Political, states and administrative districts. Covers Central and North Europe. 64 x 48 in. Cloth mounting, wood moldings and tie $19.75. Cloth mounting, spring roller and steel board $25.00. Steel case $28.00.
Excellent for authenticity and visibility.

Bild- und Lesetafel. Hahnsche, Hannover. Distr. Adler. Shows objects. Labeled in German. 66 pictures (8 x 12 in.) and 66 cards (8 x 4 in.). Posterboard $2.95.
Pictures and cards of convenient size. Used together with Dohrmann Fibel, but can be used independently.

SONGS

Deutsches Liederbuch. Jacob Hieble, (ed.). Thrift, 1948. Piano accompaniment. 32 pp. Paper $0.30.
Contains 32 songs, including carols and recent songs from different regions of Germany.

Erich Kunz Sings German University Songs. With Chorus and Vienna State Opera Orchestra. Vanguard, 1956. Four 12 in. 33⅓ rpm. discs. $4.98 each. Texts in German and English.
Student and folksongs, sung with verve and enthusiasm. Enunciation clear. Chorus, soloist and orchestra well matched.

Lieder für die Deutsche Klasse. Bowmar Record, 1960. Sung by Wolfgang Koestler. Accompanied by piano, violin, accordion and bass. One 12 in. 33⅓ rpm. disc $4.95. Includes song book by Ruth De Cesare. 19 songs. Piano accompaniment. Paper. Extra copies $1.00 each.
Well-known folksongs. Excellent diction, good range for high-school voices.

Immortal Folksongs of Germany. Performed by chorus and orchestra. London High Fidelity. Distr. London Rec. One 12 in. 33⅓ rpm. disc. $4.98. Text.
Presents many of the old favorites such as "In einem kühlen Grunde," "Aennchen von Tharau," etc.

Berühmte Kinderchöre. Folksongs. Performed by Bielefelder Kinderchor and others. Telefunken, Germany. Distr. Mielke. One 10 in. 33⅓ rpm. disc. $3.98.

Some of the songs are particularly suitable for 1–3 group, others 4–6 and some for Jr. High. There is no accompanying text.

Heimat- und Wanderlieder. Folksongs. Hauck, RIAS-Motetten-Chor. RIAS Männerchor. Akkordeon-Orchester Möncke. Europäischer. Phonoklub Recorded in Germany. One 10 in. 33⅓ rpm. disc $4.50.

A fine collection of popular *Wanderlieder,* accompanied by typical mandolin and accordion orchestra.

Christmas Songs in German. Society for Visual Education. One 12 in. 33⅓ rpm. disc. 15 min. Filmstrip and record $8.00. Record $5.00. Filmstrip $3.00. Teacher's Guide.

Nine well-known German carols, clearly sung by male and female voices. Color filmstrip with legible text. French carols on reverse of record.

Hebrew

METHODS AND MATERIALS

Hebrew in Colleges and Universities. Judah Lapson, (ed.). National Hebrew Culture Council, 1958. 155 pp. $2.00. Paper $1.00.

Useful list. Annotations give course offerings.

Bibliographiah L'Nosim B'Horaha (Madrich Lakitoth Ha-Nemuchoth Ul'Gan Ha-Yeladim). Reiter-Zedek, Miriam. Hotsoath Histadruth Ha-Morim Ha-Ivrim B'Yisrael, 1952. Distr. Rabinowitz. 798 pp. $4.00.

This handbook for teachers is especially valuable in the elementary grades, but it can also be useful to the secondary-school teacher. Stories, poems, songs, proverbs, riddles, anecdotes, and illustrative materials. Entirely in Hebrew; no index.

Hebrew Abstracts. Katsch, Abraham I. (ed.). National Assn. of Professors of Hebrew. Semi-annual, 1954– . About 30 pp. 10 x 7 in. $1.00 and issue.

Brief descriptions of articles, books, and periodicals published in all languages about the Hebrew language. Literature, philology, exegesis, bibliography and methodology. Arranged by subject. These booklets will keep the teacher informed about all important publications in the field.

"Current Trends in the Study of Hebrew in Colleges and Universities." Katsh, Abraham I. Modern Language Journal XLIV, No. 2 (Feb. 1960). $0.65.

A supplement to the information in his *Hebrew Language.*

A Bibliography of Methods and Materials of Teaching Hebrew in the Light of Recent Modern Language Methodology. Zeldner, Max. Rev. and enl. Jewish Education Com., 1958. 117 pp. Paper $2.50.

A comprehensive view of all topics relating to the teaching of Hebrew as a living language.

Hebrew Language, Literature and Culture in American Institutions of Higher Learning. Katsh, Abraham I. Payne Education Soc. Foundation, 1950. 2nd ed. 92 pp. Paper $1.00.

The only really good survey of Hebrew studies in U.S. colleges and graduate schools.

FILMS AND FILMSTRIPS

Israel. Encyclopaedia Britannica Films. $36.00. Color. $103.20. In English.

The Earth Sings. Written, directed and photographed by Sidney Lubow and others. Filmed in Israel. Montage Films, 1953. Distr. Brandon. 16 mm. 14 min. Songs in Hebrew. B. & w. Purchase $85.00. Rental $5.00 a day.

A visualization of 7 popular Hebrew songs with a montage of pastoral scenes in Israel. Beautiful photography and excellent singing of Israeli songs. Inspirational and entertaining.

Three Girls. Produced and photographed by Lasar Dunner. Filmed in Israel. Distr. Israel Film Center, 1958. 16 mm. 17 min. Dialogue in English. Color. Rental free.

A charming and absorbing film of the holiday adventures of three youthful Israelis. Fine panoramic views of Israel. Shows normal aspects of Israeli life and the refreshing vitality of Israeli youth.

SONGS

Folk Songs of Israel. Performed by Theodore Bikel. Elektra, 1955. One 12 in. 33⅓ rpm. disc. $4.98.

One of the first albums recorded by Theodore Bikel, the popular actor and folk singer. It contains 13 Israeli folk songs, several of which are based on selections from the Song of Songs. There are love songs, shepherd's melodies and lullabies. Bikel is at his best in this delightful and tastefully produced album.

Living Hebrew. Samuel Steinberg. Performed by Moshe Genser, Yoel Silberg, and Dola Ben-Yehuda Wittman. Crown, 1958. Four 10 in. 33⅓ rpm. discs $9.95. Full conversation manual with exercises and grammatical explanations and two-way dictionary.

Contains all the 40 conversation lessons in the manual *Living Hebrew.* The Israeli narrators speak clearly and distinctly and serve as good models. The pauses are uneven; frequently there is not nearly enough time for repetition. The material in the early lessons is rather dull but improves in the later lessons.

Reading in the Teaching of Hebrew. Eisenberg, Azriel, (ed.). Jewish Education Com., 1961. 297 pp. Paper $3.50.

Presents views of knowledgeable people on all aspects of the teaching of Hebrew. Aims and methods, experimentation and vocabulary selections. Sample tests and a listing of audio-visual materials.

Modern Hebrew. Rieger, Eliezer. Philosophical Library, 1953. 156 pp. $3.75.

Can be used by teachers for all age groups. An excellent presentation of most common errors and correct forms, a scholarly discussion of methodology in language instruction, and a very good listing of the basic vocabulary and cognate forms.

Darkai Limmud L'Shonenu, 2nd ed. Scharfstein, Zevi. Shilo Publishing House, 1941. 301 pp. $4.00.

Abounds in material help to the teacher. An excellent outline of ways to encourage student activities which induce language learning.

MAPS

Map of Israel. JAI, 1956. Text in English. Colored. Physical. 17 x 31 in. Paper $1.00.

Italian

COURSES

Linguaphone Conversational Course in Italian. Read by native language teachers and radio announcers. Linguaphone. Sixteen 7 in. 45 rpm. dics $57.50, with texts and case. Scholl tape programs. Thirty-two 3¾ ips. two-track tape reels, one track recorded $240.00. Set includes a Teacher's Guide and four manuals (illustrated situation manual, vocabulary list, explanatory manual, and grammar), and a carrying case. Set of first three student manuals $5.00. Grammar $1.50.

Pictures and conversation well-integrated. Uninterrupted flow of speech at normal tempo. Can serve as advanced comprehension drill.

Italian for Children. Frederick D. Eddy, (ed.). Ottenheimer. Two 10 in. 33⅓ discs $4.95. Manual with translations.

The diction is good; the material is interesting.

Conversaphone Children's Language Course. Conversaphone, 1957. One 10 in. 33⅓ rpm. disc $2.98. Manual.

Conversational Italian for lower elementary grades. Pauses for responses. Male and female voices.

Circling the Globe with Speech. Wilmac. One 12 in. 33⅓ rpm. disc $5.95. One 7 in. 7½ ips. dual-track tape with text $8.95.

Six students from various regions of Italy describe their experiences. The content is interesting.

Self-Teaching Record Course; Italian. Berlitz. Ten 12 in. discs $75.00.

Living Language Course, Italian. Crown. One 10 in. disc $6.07.

Contains basic words and expressions for everyday use.

Living Language, Italian. Columbia. Four 10 in. discs $6.07.

Begins with vowel sounds; leads up to sustained conversations.

A-LM Italian: Level One. Mary P. Thompson, Daniel P. Dato. Harcourt, 1961. Student Text (15 booklets, including index). $1.86. Teaching Tests $0.36. Student Binder $1.50. Practice Record Set, fourteen 7 in. 33⅓ rpm. discs $5.55. Classroom/Laboratory Record Set, fifteen 12 in. 33⅓ rpm. discs $30.00. Classroom/Laboratory Tape Set, thirty-six 5 in. 3¾ ips. reels $75.00 or eighteen 7 in. 7½ ips. reels $60.00. (Classroom/Laboratory discs and tapes have identical contents.) Teacher's Manual and Teacher's Desk Materials (Student Binder, one set of Student Text booklets, control sheets, Audio Index, and Teaching Tests) free to purchasers. 7½ ips. Classroom/Laboratory Tape Set available on special request for loan for copying.

TEACHERS' GUIDES

Foreign Language Revision Program for Secondary Schools. Italian. Levels I and II. New York City Board of Education. Curriculum Bulletin. September 1962. 63 pp. Paper. $1.00.

Prepared by a committee under the chairmanship of Theodore Huebener. Describes the latest materials and procedures in detail.

Italian in the Elementary Schools. Curriculum Bulletin. 1965–66 series. No. 9. 95 pp. Paper.

An excellent outline of a FLES program in Italian.

FILMS AND SLIDES

Italian Feature Films. Brandon. 16 mm. B & W. English subtitles. Rental $22.50 to $75.00. *Ladri di Bicicletti.* Directed by Vittorio de Sica. Written by Cesare Zavattini. Based on a novel by Luigi Bartolini. 1949. 87 min. *Roma, città aperta.* Directed by Roberto Rossellini. Starring Anna Magnani and others. 1945. 103 min. *Il Tetto.* Directed by Vittorio de Sica. 91 min. And other films. Excellent films. Entertaining as well as of cultural value.

Italy: Peninsula of Contrasts. The influence of physical geography upon the lives of the inhabitants. Comparison of ancient and modern cities. 17 min. Color. $168.00. Encyclopaedia Britannica Films. In English.

Italian Peninsula. Everyday life in Italy; regional occupations. 11 min. $55.00. Color. $100.00. Encyclopaedia Britannica Films.

Colored Slides on Italy. Wolfe. 35 mm. About 700 slides. Captions in English. Color. $0.45 each, 1–9 slides; $0.43 each, 10–24 slides; $0.40 each, 25–49 slides; $0.38 each, 50–99 slides; $0.35 each, 100–249 slides; $0.33 each, 250 or more. Catalogue.

Many classifications: geography, art, history, etc.

Everyday Life in Italy. Consultant W. M. Spooner. Director E. M. T. Campbell. Filmed in Italy. Educational Productions, Yorkshire, 1959. Distr. EAV. 35 mm. 41 frames. No captions. Color $5.95. Notes for the teacher describe each filmstrip in detail.

Contrasts and diversities in Italian life and geography. Accompanying notes in English.

SONGS

Italian Songs. Performed by a vocalist, pianist or accordionist. Zimelco, 1961. Recorded in U.S. Five 5 in. 3¾ ips. two-track plastic tape reels. One track recorded. Also available 7½ ips. $5.00 per reel. Text.

Each tape contains five folk songs, selected and arranged in order of linguistic and musical difficulty. Vocal plus musical accompaniment presented in a singable key. Small reels for easy use.

Yellow runner at beginning of each reel allows the teacher to follow numbering of song text for fast identification.

Songs of Old Italy. Sung by Maria Terrana. Guitar by Carlo Martines. Folk songs. Playette, 1957. One 12 in. 33⅓ rpm. disc $5.95. Text. Extra copies $0.10 each.

Ten folk songs delightfully sung in Tuscan Italian. Excellent for supplementing classwork and for use in clubs.

Italian Sing-Along. Performed by The Italian Street Singers with orchestra. Popular Italian songs. Decca, n.d. One 12 in. 33⅓ rpm. disc $3.98.

Five free lyric sheets of the words; no melody text. Contents "Santa Lucia," "O Sole Mio," "Oh, Marie," "Ciribiribin," "Arrivederci Roma," etc.

Italian Folksongs and Dances. Recorded in Italy. Folkways, 1955. One 10 in. 33⅓ rpm. disc $4.25.

Solo and choral songs and instrumental. Charming and entertaining selections principally from Southern Italy, Sicily and Sardinia.

Canzoni per la classe d'italiano. Bowmar Record, 1961. One 12 in. 33⅓ rpm. disc $4.95. Includes songbook by Ruth De Cesare. 17 pp. Paper. Extra copies $1.00 each.

Sixteen songs from various sections of Italy. Cumulative vocabularies provided for all songs.

MAPS AND CHARTS

Italy, Physical-Political. De Agostini, 1960. Distr. Denoyer. Text in Italian. Colored. 71 x 83 in. Cloth mounting, wood moldings and tie $25.00. Cloth mounting, spring roller and steel board $31.50. Well done; excellent colors.

Italy, Physical-Political. Paravia, 1955. Distr. Denoyer. Text in Italian. Colored. 39 x 55 in. Cloth mounting, wood moldings and tie $10.75. Cloth mounting, spring roller and steel board $13.75. Very good coloring.

Russian

COURSES

Living Russian. Read by Aron Pressman. Living, 1958. Conversation Manual and dictionary. Four 10 in. 33⅓ rpm discs $9.95. Extra manuals and dictionaries $1.50 each.

Another version of the Holt Spoken Language series. Suitable as a course for adults rather than for high school students.

A–LM Russian: Level One. Mary P. Thompson and Marina Prochoroff. Harcourt, 1961. Student text (15 booklets, including index). $1.86. Teaching Tests $0.36. Student Binder $1.50. Practice Record Set, fourteen 7 in. $33\frac{1}{3}$ rpm. discs $5.55. Classroom/Laboratory Record Set, fifteen 12 in. $33\frac{1}{3}$ rpm. discs $30.00. Classroom/Laboratory Tape Set, thirty-six 5 in. $3\frac{3}{4}$ ips. reels $75.00, or eighteen 7 in. $7\frac{1}{2}$ ips. reels $60.00. Classroom/Laboratory discs and tapes have identical contents. Teacher's Manual and Teacher's Desk Materials (Student Binder, one set of Student Text booklets, control sheets, Audio Index, and Teaching Tests) free to purchasers.

Content of Level I best suited for junior high school. Some units may not hold student interest. Discs must be handled manually. Diction good.

Russian Language and Civilization. Birkmaier, Emma. A four-year course. Bulletin No. 1, Univ. of Minnesota. Birkmaier, 1958, 48 pp. Mimeographed $1.00.

The syllabus with its suggestions for use of texts and films is valuable for teachers of Russian. The program is too difficult, however, for the average high school.

Russian, Levels I and II, III, IV. 3 vols. Board of Education of the City of New York. Parts I and II, 1962, 63 pp. Part III, 1963, 69 pp. Part IV, 1964, 69 pp. Paper, $1.00 each.

Useful for the experienced teacher. Many excellent suggestions for the effective use of audio-visual aids are given. The cultural outline is excellent. The program is rather heavy in grammatical items.

FILMS AND SLIDES

Rest and Leisure in the USSR. Consultants: Olga S. Federoff and Walter I. Bond. Filmed in USSR. International Film Bureau, 1963. 16 mm. 14 min. Narrated. Color. Purchase $150.00. Rental $7.50. Text.

Excellent presentation of the activities of the Russian citizen in his spare time. Depicts both children and adults during leisure hours and vacation. The language is simple and the photography vivid.

My Name is Ivan. Also known as *Ivan's Childhood*. Directed by Andrei Tartovsky. Filmed in USSR. Brandon, 1962. 16 mm. 84 min. Dialogue. Subtitles. B & W. Apply for price.

The story of a boy who lost his parents in war. He lives with a group of soldiers at the front and serves as scout and companion. Warm human relationship. Fine film with emotional content.

Moscow and Leningrad. One of four graded language films. Consultants: Olga S. Federoff and Walter I. Bond. Filmed in USSR. International Film Bureau, 1963. 16 mm. 14 min. Narrated. Color. Purchase $150.00. Rental $7.50. Text.

A very attractive presentation of Moscow and Leningrad. Narration uses simple vocabulary for description of the two cities. Can be used effectively both for language and culture.

Russian Poetry. Read by Larissa Gatora. Folkways. One 12 in. 33⅓ rpm. disc $5.95. Extra text $0.50.

Excellent choice of poems, read clearly. The print of the accompanying text is rather small. English translation.

Russian for Children. Frederick D. Eddy, (ed.). Spoken by children and adults. Ottenheimer, 1959. Two 10 in. 33⅓ rpm. discs $4.95. Russian and English texts and a manual for teachers and parents. Excellent recording; good voices. Fine introduction for children of lower grades; may be used in both 1st and 2nd years.

Gateway to Russian. Frederick D. Eddy, (ed.). Ottenheimer, 1960. Two 12 in. 33⅓ rpm. discs $7.95. Conversational manual and alphabetical phrase index.

Excellent for students who plan to visit the Soviet Union. Expressions particularly useful for the traveler.

SONGS

Russian Songs for Teaching Russian. Sung by Getta Petry. Guitar accompaniment. Folkways, 1960. One 12 in. 33⅓ rpm. disc $5.95. Russian and English text. Extra text $0.50.

Good children's songs, including some from the Soviet period. Singer reads words first and then sings. Suitable for all ages.

Russian Hymns and Carols. Sung by the Russian Orthodox Cathedral Choir of Paris. Monitor. One 12 in. 33⅓ rpm. disc. Mono and stereo. $4.98. Includes Russian text and English translations on jacket.

Because of the Old Church Slavic elements in the language of the songs, it would be difficult to use these records in class, but they can be used to advantage in the Russian Club.

Moussorgsky Melodies. Sung by Boris Christoff. Angel. Four 12 in. 33⅓ rpm. discs $4.98 each. Text.

Excellent supplementary material suitable for Russian clubs. Soloist exceptionally clear. Accompanying book quite beautiful, containing complete text in Russian, English, French and Italian. Contains many vivid illustrations of cultural significance.

Russian Folk Songs. Soloists and choral groups. Recorded in Europe. Vanguard, 1958. One 12 in. 33⅓ rpm. disc $4.98.

Good singing, excellent diction. Old folk songs and some new Soviet songs of a non-political nature. Mimeographed text.

Spanish

TEACHERS' GUIDES

Curriculum Guide for Spanish. Board of Education. City of Chicago. Chicago Ed., 1964. 254 pp. Paper $2.50.

This valuable guide for the Spanish teacher is designed to implement audio-lingual methods and techniques from the 7th grade through the 12th. Its 27 chapters are detailed and comprehensive.

Beginning Spanish in Grade Three. Modern Language Association. Teacher's Guide. Educ. Pub., 1958. 50 pp. Paper $2.50. One 12 in. 33⅓ rpm. disc. $5.00.

A course in conversational Spanish for children, exemplifying modern methodology. Very useful, although voices are sometimes abrupt and harsh, making syllables indistinct.

Continuing Spanish in Grade Five. Modern Language Association. Teacher's Guide. Educ. Pub., 1958. 76 pp. Paper $2.50. One 12 in. 33⅓ rpm. disc $5.00.

Excellent illustration of newer methods and materials.

Continuing Spanish in Grade Six. Modern Language Association. Teacher's Guide. Educ. Pub., 1960. 50 pp. Paper $2.50. MLA Student's Book for Spanish in Grade Six (Reading Units 1–7) $1.00.

Illustrative of newer methods and materials.

Continuing Spanish in Grade Four. Modern Language Association. Teacher's Guide. Educ. Pub., 1958. 55 pp. Paper $2.50. One 12 in. 33⅓ rpm. disc $5.00.

A course guide to follow beginning Spanish in Grade 3. Good.

Teaching Spanish: A Linguistic Orientation. Politzer, Robt. L., and Charles N. Staubach. Ginn, 1961. 136 pp. Paper $3.00.

An examination of the specific contribution that linguistics can make to the teacher of beginning Spanish in high school or college. Selected bibliography.

Teaching Spanish in the Grades. MacRae, Margit W. Houghton, 1957. 408 pp. $5.00. Two 12 in. 33⅓ rpm. discs $15.00. Texts: Spanish in the Grades. Book One: Mi cuaderno de español $0.88. Teacher's edition $3.00. Book Two: Mi cuaderno de español $0.88. Teacher's edition $3.00.

Excellent presentation of the story-telling method. Does not do justice to dialogue method. Detailed suggestion on guides, materials and procedures. Begin in grade 3, 4, or 5.

Foreign Language Revision Program for Secondary Schools. Spanish. Levels I and II. Curriculum Bulletin 1962–63 series. No. 2B. New York City Board of Education, 1962. 76 pp. Paper $1.00.

Produced by an impressive committee of language teachers. Reflects the latest thinking with reference to methodology and materials.

———, Level IV. 1964. 38 pp. Paper $1.00.

Excellent content; unusually helpful.

———, Level III. 1963. 74 pp. Paper $1.00.

Detailed outlines of work for this level.

———, *Spanish in the Elementary Schools.* Grades 4, 5, and 6. Curriculum Bulletin 1961–62 Series. No. 14. 1963. 98 pp. Paper $1.00.

Comprehensive, thorough and well-planned.

Spanish in the Elementary Schools. Grades 4-5-6. New York City Board of Education. Curriculum Bulletin 1961–62 series. No. 14. 98 pp. Paper.

An excellent outline of an elementary school program in Spanish.

COURSES

Living Language Course: Spanish. Crown. One 10 in. disc $6.07.

Letters and sounds of Spanish; lists of words, sentences and dialogues.

Self-Teaching Record Course: Spanish. Berlitz. Ten 12 in. discs $75.00.

Circling the Globe with Speech: Spanish II. Wilmac. One 12 in. disc $5.60.

Anecdotes and descriptions of the following: Merida, Madrid, Valencia, Montevideo, Buenos Aires, Santiago, etc.

FILMS AND FILMSTRIPS

Un Viaje a México. Encyclopaedia Britannica Films. 11 min. Color. $120.00.
  Narrative in slowly spoken Spanish.
Madrid. International Film Bureau. Color. Spanish. 11 min. $100.00.
  Field trip to Madrid. Excellent dialogue.
Highlands of the Andes. United World Films. English and Spanish. 20 min. $100.00.
  Detailed account of life in the Andes with scenes of Cuzco and Lima.
La vida en un pueblo mexicano. Filmed in Mexico. Hoeffler, dist. Disney, 1960. 16 mm. 17 min. Narrated in Spanish. Color. Purchase $160.00. Teacher's Guide.
  Beautiful photography. Presents daily activities.
Un pueblo de España. Script by Charles N. Butt; narrated by Manuel Paris. Directed by Gunther V. Fritsch. Filmed in Spain. Churchill, 1958. 16 mm. 12 min. Narrated in Spanish. Color. Purchase $115.00; rental $5.00. B & W purchase $65.00; rental $3.50. One 5 in. 7½ ips. plastic single-track tape reel. 7 min. Recorded by Victor Perrin.
  The schoolmaster's view of life in a village in southern Spain. School, church and family; emphasis on the latter. Voice clear.
People of Spain. Encyclopaedia Britannica Films. 16 min. $90.00. Color $180.00.
  A history of the cultures that have influenced the development of Spain. In English.
Spanish Conquest of the New World. Coronet Instructional Films. 11 min. $55.00. Color $110.00.
  The deeds of the Spanish explorers and colonizers. In English.
España: Una familia de Valencia. Spanish narration by Joseph Raymond. Filmed in Spain. Frith, 1960. 16 mm. 16 min. Color. Purchase $136.00. Script.
  Informative and entertaining.
Vamos a España: Parts I, II, and III. Each $3.50. Gessler.
  Spanish cities (Madrid, Toledo, Avila, Sevilla, Granada, etc.) from a cultural and historical point of view.

168

Una familia de un pueblo mexicano. Filmed in Mexico. Hoeffler, dist. Disney, 1960. 16 mm. 17 min. Narration in Spanish. Color. Purchase $160.00. Study guide.

Life in a small Mexican village. A realistic picture of a poor family which presents not only the hardships but also the pleasures of village life.

Spanish for Elementary Schools. Consultant Vera Villegas. McGraw Films, 1959–60. Each set has 6 color filmstrips, three 10 in. 33⅓ rpm. discs, and a teacher's manual. Each strip presents frames, once without captions and once with Spanish captions. Each set $57.50.

Teacher's Guide has many helpful suggestions. The vocabulary is simple and basic.

México trabajando. Consultant Margit MacRae. Filmed in Mexico. Hoeffler, 1960. 16 mm. 17 min. Narration in Spanish. Color. Purchase $160.00. Script, Teacher's Guide, questions for discussion, suggested activities.

Elementary Spanish for Young Americans. Consultants José Sanchez and Audrey Castillo. Filmed in U.S. Society for Visual Education, 1961. 35 mm. Set of 6 filmstrips with three 12 in. 33⅓ rpm. discs. Photographs. Color. Purchase $35.10. Reading script and utilization guide.

Shows a boy and a girl in everyday situations at home and in school. Useful for beginning classes in junior high school. Tempo is slow.

Don Quijote (Parts I and II) and *El Cid Campeador.* Filmed in Spain. Produced by Ancora. Distr. Escopel. 35 mm. 35 frames. $5.50 each strip.

Excellent for enrichment. Dramatized episodes in brilliant color.

Circling the Globe with Speech: Spanish. Vol. I. Dialogues. Wilmac, 1961. One 12 in. 33⅓ rpm. disc. 52 min. $5.95 or one 7 in. 7½ ips. dual-track tape. $8.95. Texts.

Dialogues based on visits to Spanish-speaking countries. The speakers are high school students. At times the conversation seems to be somewhat stilted.

SONGS

Spain, An Anthology of Spanish Folk Music. Vol. I. Recorded in Spain. Monitor. One 12 in. 33⅓ rpm. disc. 47 min. $4.98. Text $0.50.

Collection of folk-songs sung by non-professional artists. Jotas, fandangos, rondas and seguidillas. Accompanying text with free translations. Good as cultural material.

Mexican Songs. Recorded in Mexico. RCA. 15 discs. $3.32 each.
Series of records with six popular Mexican songs on each side. Sung by popular artists accompanied by orchestra.

Christmas Songs of Spain. Recorded by Laura Boulton. Castanet and tambourine accompaniment. Recorded in Spain. Folkways, 1955. One 10 in. 33⅓ rpm. disc $4.25. Text and notes.
Spanish Christmas carols sung by children and adults.

Canciones para la clase de español. Guitar, marimba and piano accompaniment. Bowmar Records, 1960. One 12 in. 33⅓ rpm. disc $4.95. Songbook by Ruth De Cesare. Piano accompaniment with guitar notations. 17 pp. Paper. Extra copies $1.00.
Seventeen Spanish songs sung by native voices; clear and pleasant. The "sing along" style is employed. All the songs are easy to sing. An end vocabulary is provided.

Cancionero Infantil. Piano and organ. Spanish Music Center, 1958. One 12 in. 33⅓ rpm. disc $4.95. Text.
Although the songs were chosen from those used on a children's radio program in Mexico, they are suitable for older students.

Canciones de España. Sung by Germaine Montero, Salvator Bacaresse; accompanied by orchestra. Recorded in U.S. Vanguard, 1956. One 12 in. 33⅓ rpm. disc $4.98. Text.
An excellent selection which can be used in all grades.

Songs, Dances of Puerto Rico. Folkways. One 12 in. disc $3.63.
Songs and dances performed by native artists, using native instruments.

LITERATURE

Golden Treasury of Spanish Verse. Read by Ricardo Florit. Spoken Arts, 1962. One 12 in. 33⅓ rpm. disc $5.95. Script.
A good selection of major Spanish poets. Clearly presented.

The Golden Treasury of Spanish-American Verse. Read by Manual Durán. Spoken Arts, 1962. One 12 in. 33⅓ rpm. disc $5.95. Script and biographies of authors.
Selections from the works of 15 distinguished Latin-American poets.

Professional Journals

The Modern Language Journal. Published by the National Federation of Modern Language Teachers Associations. Business Manager: Wallace G. Klein, 13149 Cannes Drive, St. Louis, Mo. 63141.

The French Review. Published by the American Association of Teachers of French. Secretary-Treasurer: J. Henry Owens, Eastern Michigan University, Ypsilanti, Mich. 48197.

The German Quarterly. Published by the American Association of Teachers of German. Business Manager: Herbert H. J. Peisel, Syracuse University, Syracuse, N. Y. 13210.

Hispania. Published by the American Association of Teachers of Spanish and Portuguese. Secretary-Treasurer: Eugene Savaiano, Wichita State University, Wichita, Kansas. 67208.

Italica. Quarterly Bulletin of the American Association of Teachers of Italian. Secretary-Treasurer: Ernest S. Falbo, Gonzaga University, Spokane, Wash. 99202.

Service Bureaus

French Cultural Services. 972 Fifth Ave., New York, N.Y. 10021.

A.A.T.F. National Information Bureau. Director: Armand Begué, Brooklyn College, Brooklyn, New York. 11210.

A.A.T.G. Service Bureau. Glenn Waas, Colgate University, Hamilton, N.Y. 13346.

National Hebrew Culture Council. Judah Lapson. 426 W. 58th St., New York, N.Y. 10019.

Italian Language Service Bureau. Secretary-Treasurer: John Cardillo. Casa Italiana, 117th & Amsterdam Ave., New York, N.Y. 10027.

American Association for the Advancement of Slavic Studies. Secretary: Ralph T. Fisher, Jr., 337 Lincoln Hall, University of Illinois, Urbana, Ill. 61801.

PRODUCERS AND SUPPLIERS

The following list gives the addresses of producers and suppliers of products listed in the above bibliography, with the exception of major publishers of books and records, whose products may be purchased through normal retail or wholesale sources. Many of the organizations listed below will supply catalogs on request, which will list a far greater variety of materials than it was possible to include in this selective bibliography.

Academy Films, P.O. Box 3088, Hollywood, Cal. 90028
Adlers Foreign Books, 110 W. 47 St., New York, N.Y. 10036
Allen Moore Productions, Inc., 213 W. 7 St., Los Angeles, Cal. 90015
Almanac Films, 29 E. 10 St., New York, N.Y. 10003
American Council on Education, 1785 Massachusetts Ave., N.W., Washington, D.C. 20036
American Film Producers, 1600 Broadway, New York, N.Y. 10036
American Museum of Natural History, Central Park West at 74 St., New York, N.Y. 10024
Assimil, 610 Fifth Ave., New York, N.Y. 10020
Association Films, 347 Madison Ave., New York, N.Y. 10017
Audio-Master Co., 17 E. 45 St., New York, N.Y. 10017
Audio-Visual Associates, 2161 Milburn Ave., Baldwin, N.Y. 11510
Bailey Films, Inc., 6509 De Longpre Ave., Hollywood, Cal. 90028
Barr Productions, 1265 Bresee Ave., Pasadena, Cal. 90004
Berlitz Publications, 630 Fifth Ave., New York, N.Y. 10020
Birkmaier, Emma, University High School, Univ. of Minnesota, Minneapolis, Minn. 55455
Bowmar, Stanley, 12 Cleveland St., Valhalla, N.Y. 10595
Bowmar Records, 4921 Santa Monica Blvd., Los Angeles, Cal. 90029
Brandon Films, 200 W. 57 St., New York, N.Y. 10019
Bray Studios, 729 Seventh Ave., New York, N.Y. 10019
Broadcasting and Film Commission, 475 Riverside Dr., New York, N.Y. 10027
Caedmon Records, 277 Fifth Ave., New York, N.Y. 10016
Capitol Records, Hollywood & Vine, Hollywood, Cal. 90028
Casterman, Editions, 66 Rue Bonaparte, Paris 6e, France
Carillon Records, 520 Fifth Ave., New York, N.Y. 10036
Children's Music Center, 2858 W. Pico Blvd., Los Angeles, Cal. 90006
Church Screen Productions, P.O. Box 5036, Nashville, Tenn. 37206
Churchill Films, 6671 Sunset Blvd., Los Angeles, Cal. 90028
Columbia Records, 799 Seventh Ave., New York, N.Y. 10019

Columbia University, Teachers College, 525 W. 120 St., New York, N.Y. 10027

Columbia University Press, 2960 Broadway, New York, N.Y. 10027

Coronet Films, 488 Madison Ave., New York, N.Y. 10022

Conversaphone Institute, 2 E. 23 St., New York, N.Y. 10010

Cortina Academy, 136 W. 52 St., New York, N.Y. 10019

Decca Records, 445 Park Ave., New York, N.Y. 10010

Denoyer-Geppert Co., 5235 Ravenswood Ave., Chicago, Ill. 60640

Dover Publications, 920 Broadway, New York, N.Y. 10010

Disney, Walt, Productions, Educational Film Div., 500 S. Buena Vista Ave., Burbank, Cal. 91505

Educational Audio-Visual, 29 Marble Ave., Pleasantville, N.Y. 10570

Educational Film Library Association, 250 W. 57 St., New York, N.Y. 10019

Educational Publishing Co., 23 Leroy Ave., Darien, Conn. 06820

Educational Services, 1730 I St., N.W., Washington, D.C. 20006

Elektra Records, 116 W. 14 St., New York, N.Y. 10011

Encyclopaedia Britannica Films, 202 E. 42 St., New York, N.Y. 10017

EMC Recording Co., 806 E. 7 St., St. Paul, Minn. 55106

Epic Recordings, 35 W. 45 St., New York, N.Y. 10036

Escopel Co., P.O. Box 320, Montclair, N.J. 07042

Europäischer Phonoklub, Silberburgstrasse 150, Stuttgart, W. Germany

Eye Gate House, 146-01 Archer Ave., Jamaica, Queens, N.Y. 11435

FACSEA, 972 Fifth Ave., New York, N.Y. 10021 (Lending library).

Film Images, Inc., 220 W. 42 St., New York, N.Y. 10036

Films of Nations, 62 W. 45 St., New York, N.Y. 10036

Filmfax Productions, 80 W. 40 St., New York, N.Y. 10018

Filmstrip House, 432 Park Ave., S., New York, N.Y. 10003

Focus Films Co., 1385 Westwood Blvd., Los Angeles, Cal. 90024

Folkways, 165 W. 46 St., New York, N.Y. 10036

French Film Office, 645 Madison Ave., New York, N.Y. 10021

Frith Films, 1816 N. Highland Ave., Hollywood, Cal. 90028

Funk & Wagnalls, 153 W. 24 St., New York, N.Y. 10010

Gateway Productions, Inc., 1859 Powell St., San Francisco, Cal. 94110

General Pictures Productions, 621 Sixth Ave., Des Moines, Iowa. 50316

Gessler Publishing Co., Hastings-on-Hudson, N.Y. 13076

Goldsmith's Music Shop, 401 W. 42 St., New York, N.Y. 10036

Greystone Corp., 100 Ave. of the Americas, New York, N.Y. 10014

Hachette, 79 Boulevard St. Germain, Paris 6ᵉ, France

Harcourt, Brace, and World, 750 Third Ave., New York, N.Y. 10017

Harmon Foundation, 140 Nassau St., New York, N.Y. 10038

Hatier, 8 Rue d'Assas, Paris 7, France

Heath, D. C., and Co., 285 Columbus Ave., Boston, Mass. 02116

Heath de Rochemont Corp., 16 Arlington St., Boston, Mass. 02170

Heritage Filmstrips, 89-11 63 Dr., Rego Park, New York 11374

Hoefler Productions, see Disney.

Hoffberg Productions, Inc., 362 W. 44 St., New York, N.Y. 10018

Hollywood Film Enterprises, 6060 Sunset Blvd., Hollywood, Cal. 90028

Holt, Rinehart, and Winston, 383 Madison Ave., New York, N.Y. 10017

Ideal Pictures Corp., 65 E. South Water St., Chicago, Ill. 60601

International Business Machines, 555 Madison Ave., New York, N.Y. 10022

International Film Bureau, 332 S. Michigan Ave., Chicago, Ill. 60604

International Films, 1150 Wilmette Ave., Wilmette, Ill. 60091

International Screen, 609 Philadelphia Ave., Washington, D.C. 20012

Israeli Film Center, 515 Park Ave., New York, N.Y. 10022

Jewish Education Committee Press, 426 W. 58 St., New York, N.Y. 10019

Key Productions, 527 Madison Ave., New York, N.Y. 10022

Kleinberg, Ernest, Films, 3890 Edgeview Dr., Pasadena, Cal. 91107

Knowledge Builders, Classroom Films, 625 Madison Ave., New York, N.Y. 10022

Language Research, 13 Kirkland St., Cambridge, Mass. 02138

Language Training Aids, Boyds, Md. 20720

Linguaphone Institute, 30 Rockefeller Plaza, New York, N.Y. 10020

Life Magazine Filmstrips, Time-Life Building, Rockefeller Plaza, New York, N.Y. 10020

Living Language Course, 100 Ave. of the Americas, New York, N.Y. 10013

Lorraine Music Co., P.O. Box 4131, Long Island City, Queens, New York, 11104

McGraw-Hill Book Co., 330 W. 42 St., New York, N.Y. 10036

McGraw-Hill Text-Film Dept., 330 W. 42 St., New York, N.Y. 10036

Mahnke, Carl F., Productions, 215 E. 3 St., Des Moines, Iowa. 50309

Mentor Records, 501 Madison Ave., New York, N.Y. 10022

Mielke, H., Co., 242 E. 86 St., New York, N.Y. 10028

Modern Film Corp., 729 Seventh Ave., New York, N.Y. 10019

Modern Talking Pictures Service, 10 Rockefeller Plaza, New York, N.Y. 10020

Monitor Records, 445 W. 49th St., New York, N.Y. 10019

Morthole, E. L., 8855 Lincolnwood Dr., Evanston, Ill. 60203

Movies En Route, 729 Seventh Ave., New York, N.Y. 10019

National Tape Library, 2413 Pennsylvania Ave., N.W., Washington, D.C. 20037

National Tape Recording Project, Kent State University, Kent, Ohio. 44240

New York Times, School Service Dept., 229 W. 43 St., New York, N.Y. 10036

Ottenheimer Publishers, 4805 Nelson Ave., Baltimore, Md. 21215

Pathescope Co. of America, 71 Weyman Ave., New Rochelle, New York. 10805

Payne Education Society Foundation, New York Univ., New York, N.Y. 10003

Period Records, 304 E. 74 St., New York, N.Y. 10021

Philosophical Library, 15 E. 40 St., New York, N.Y. 10016

Photo and Sound Productions, 116 Natoma St., San Francisco, Cal. 94105

Pictorial Events, 220 Central Park S., New York, N.Y. 10019

Pictura Films Corp., 29 E. 10 St., New York, N.Y. 10003

Post Pictures Corp., 445 E. 86 St., New York, N.Y. 10028

Princeton Film Center, Carter Rd., Princeton, N.J. 08540

Progressive Pictures, 6351 Thornhill Dr., Oakland, Cal. 94611

RCA Victor, Educational Division, 155 E. 24 St., New York, N.Y. 10010

The Record Hunter, 507 Fifth Ave., New York, N.Y. 10017

Regents Publishing Co., Inc., 200 Park Ave. S., New York, N.Y. 10003

Row, Peterson, and Co., 1911 Ridge Ave., Evanston, Ill. 60202

Shilo Publishing House, 88 Division St., New York, N.Y. 10002

Silver-Burdett Co., Park Ave., Morristown, N.J. 07960

Society for Visual Education, Inc., 1345 Diversey Pkwy., Chicago, Ill. 60614

Spanish Music Center, 127 W. 48 St., New York, N.Y. 10036

Spoken Arts, 95 Valley Rd., New Rochelle, N.Y. 10804

Spoken Word, 10 E. 39 St., New York, N.Y. 10016

Sterling Films, 6 E. 39 St., New York, N.Y. 10016

United World Films, Inc., 221 Park Ave. S., New York, N.Y. 10003

Vanguard Recording Society, 256 W. 55 St., New York, N.Y. 10019

Vocarium Records, 12 Rock Hill St., West Medford, Mass. 02156

Walch, J. Weston, P.O. Box 1075, Portland, Me. 04104

Wible Language Institute, Hamilton Law Building, Allentown, Pa. 18101

Wilmac Records, 921 E. Green St., Pasadena, Cal. 91101

Wolfe Worldwide Films, 1657 Sawtelle Blvd., Los Angeles, Cal. 90025

World in Color Productions, 108 W. Church St., Elmira, N.Y. 14901

Zimelco Taping Service, 156-20 101 St., Howard Beach, Queens, New York. 11414

Zodiac Recording Co., 501 Madison Ave., New York, N.Y. 10022

Index